May, 1953

With best [...]

from the [...]

for a good

convalescence —

WITH GOD IN RED CHINA

WITH GOD IN RED CHINA

With God
IN RED CHINA

The Story of Two Years in
Chinese Communist Prisons

F. OLIN STOCKWELL

HARPER & BROTHERS, PUBLISHERS
New York

WITH GOD IN RED CHINA

Copyright, 1953, by Harper & Brothers
Printed in the United States of America

All rights in this book are reserved.
No part of the book may be used or reproduced
in any manner whatsoever without written permission except in the case of brief quotations
embodied in critical articles and reviews. For
information address Harper & Brothers
49 East 33rd Street, New York 16, N. Y.

D-C

Library of Congress catalog card number: 53–6973

To the third generation, Margaret and Eugene, who will write the next chapter in missionary history

Contents

Contents

Foreword

The first nine chapters of this book were written in a prison cell in Chungking, China, on the margins of an anthology of modern poetry, *The Music Makers*, compiled by Stanton A. Coblentz. They were written at the end of the first half of what proved to be nearly two years of imprisonment at the hands of the People's Government. By what seemed like a providential act, they escaped the attention of the Communist guards who processed my luggage and were thus brought out of China as they were originally written. The last chapter, telling the story of the nine and a half months of Communist indoctrination, was written in Hong Kong immediately after my release.

This story is simply the tale of what happened in China during the high tide of revolutionary change as one missionary saw it. For several years before arrest, all books and magazines from the West came through very slowly. During the months of imprisonment, there was no contact with the outside world. For this reason, the understanding of the world struggle, the changing tides of thought and attitude, and the sequence of international events were almost entirely outside my knowledge when this story was first told. Perhaps a fuller knowledge would have made for a more perfect interpretation of world movements.

But it is hoped that the reader will be tolerant of all such faults in the story, recognizing that this is not another attempt to interpret the situation in the Far East. I have no qualifications for such a serious task. Rather, this is a story of the religious experience of one humble disciple who discovered the realities of his religious faith. The testimony given here is essentially the same that scores of missionaries and hundreds of Chinese Christians are giving today. For God is still able to take a perfectly rotten situation and transmute it into a victory march.

To my son Foster and to my wife, to my friends Roderick Scott, Frank T. Cartwright, Frank Cooley, and others who have read the manuscript and given helpful suggestions, I am heavily indebted. Unfortunately, I cannot blame them for the many errors in judgment which still remain. The shortcomings are all too obvious. But I trust the reader will find in these chapters that which I seek most to give—a witness to the sustaining power of the grace of God experienced by one who walked through dark and lonely places.

WITH GOD IN RED CHINA

WITH GOD IN RED CHINA

1

The Fall of the House of Chiang

To close more than twenty years of missionary work in China with nearly two years in a Communist jail had not been a part of my life plan. When I left my Methodist pastorate in Oklahoma back in 1929 and sailed for the Far East, with my wife and two children, I had gone to share with Chinese Christians in the task of preaching the Christian faith and building the Christian fellowship. Both in the first five years in South China and during the next fifteen years in West China, Chinese co-workers were consistently tolerant of my blunders and grateful for any friendly help. Through her quick sympathy and her musical talent my wife had won a real place in the hearts of many students and other friends. Our latchstring was always out. Chinese friends came and went, borrowing everything from a million dollars in deflated currency to the use of our bathtub, but usually compromising with an evening of fellowship or a promise for help at the next concert. Little did we dream that this lovely symphony would end on such a sour note.

The end came with the fall of the house of Chiang Kai-shek, and that collapse was completed in 1949. Our experience of that collapse began three years earlier, when we returned to China in that relic of World War II, the troopship *Marine Lynx*. So I must begin my story in October, 1946. It seems but yesterday.

I remember the *Marine Lynx* as it stolidly plowed its yellow furrow up the sluggish waters of the Whangpoo. We would be docking at the wharf in another hour and leave this overcrowded troopship that had been our home for three weeks. The first large contingent of postwar missionaries, some four hundred strong, together with about one hundred and fifty Chinese returned students, would be at the end of the first lap of their long journey. A few days later they would be fanning out in all directions, facing new opportunities and new adjustments.

It had been a good trip. The long delay of more than a month in San Francisco, due to labor trouble on the water front, had been compensated for by a kindly providence at sea. The hot and crowded quarters, with men in the center of the boat and women in the bow, sleeping and living in three-decker canvas bunks, soldier style, had been weathered with a fortitude and good cheer that augured well for the hard years before us. As head of the missionary group, all complaints came to me. A responsible committee divided up the duties, solved small problems before they became big ones, and life had been good for everyone. Of course there were minor difficulties. The ladies had no bath curtains in their shower room, which was annoying under ordinary circumstances, but became definitely embarrassing when the night watchman barged in to see if there were any evidences of fire or smoke. Some mothers complained that the milk ration for their children was not enough, so it had to be increased. Room was limited, but the recreation committee arranged for bridge tournaments in one part of the dining room and prayer meetings in another, to everyone's satisfaction.

The day before our landing everyone had been busy filling out customs forms, worried about what to declare and what to conceal, struggling between their sense of honesty and a desire to save their Boards unnecessary expense. There were rumors of exorbitant customs charges. But one missionary dowager was most comforting as she sailed up to me like a frigate, dropped her anchor, and in great confidence whispered, "I am a friend of Madame Chiang and I have written her that it would be a gesture of warm welcome to instruct the customs to waive all duties on this first contingent of returning missionaries. I am sure she will." She knew how things are done in China, but her optimism proved to be ill-founded.

The last morning was spent in rustling baggage. There were no porters or cabin boys. So that meant the married men had not only their own family baggage to carry up three flights of stairs, but that of the single women as well, a double duty that must be recognized and accepted without complaint in polygamous societies. So there was not much time to note the few steamers tied up where there had once been a whole covey of foreign gunboats or to study the occasional evidences of war damage visible across the low, flat fields. We must get all hand baggage on deck for customs inspection before docking. Then we would be free to disembark, coming back to the wharf and customs godown the next day to claim trunks and boxes. The customs inspector had been kind to me, confiscating only my radio until I could secure the proper permit to take it in. Many others were not so fortunate.

All the missionaries in Shanghai seemed to have congregated on the wharf to welcome us. They were cordial. The weather, which had threatened rain all day, was considerate and waited until midnight to weep its October tears. The coolies who moved baggage down the one narrow gangway were few, so we got a rope and lowered several hundred pieces of baggage over the side to friends below. Customs cocked a questioning eye at such unorthodox proceedings, as it gave them no chance to see if the baggage had been inspected, but decided not to interfere. We were all off the ship and in the bosom of friendly families before bedtime. Our worries were all over—or were they?

The next day was a grand melee at the customs shed. The coolies who had put trunks and boxes into the godown were supposed to stack baggage in alphabetical order so that Jones could find his belongings in the stack under "J," but having a hazy idea of the alphabet, the result was alphabet soup. So each man hunted through several thousand pieces before locating his score or more of trunks and boxes. Some spent a week on this treasure hunt; I got through the morning of the second day. Then, having assembled my stuff, I waited in line several hours for an inspector, finally found one, and was through before closing time in the afternoon. The damages were a few million Chinese dollars, less than fifty dollars U.S., and a flash gun for camera which the inspector thought would fit his own camera. I was not in a position to argue the case. I watched a Baptist brother who had a total of one hundred and fifty-two pieces, most of them in pasteboard cartons that had not stood the trip too well. He was worried because one case of grape juice had lost eleven of its twelve bottles in transit from boat to godown, and thought the customs ought to replace these. The inspector was equally worried, not over the grape juice, but over a customs declaration that was such a mass of undecipherable scrawl that neither he nor anyone else could calculate the duty charges. When I left they were still fighting on different battle fronts.

Esther, Ed, and Jean took the plane a few days later to Chungking. Esther is my wife, and I shall say no more for fear of saying either too little or too much. Ed and Jean

17

are the Knettlers, who hail from Drew Seminary and were going to West China as new recruits of the Methodist mission. He had specialized in rural evangelism and has that thorough German mind which enabled him to get more Chinese language, both spoken and written, in his ensuing five years of service than I had acquired in twenty. His wife plays second fiddle with distinguished grace and skill, as many wives do.

I stayed in Shanghai to see about the baggage but after days of walking the streets, I turned the whole of our luggage over to China Travel Service to move to West China, in spite of the warnings of friends that it would be pilfered en route. Their fears proved groundless, for it got through without loss. A later shipment came through in the same way, including even a crate of ten-foot lengths of water pipe, paint, mop, hoe, spade, rake, and broom arriving without the loss of an item. Only the crate was missing, probably confiscated by the coolies as their legitimate squeeze. I agreed with them, though, being gentlemen, we did not discuss the matter.

I, too, took a plane to Chungking. As we soared over the rice fields of the Shanghai delta, my mind went back over the war years, a tale that was drawing to a close when I had left China eighteen months earlier. We had been fortunate to get out of China early in 1941, before Japan forced America into the war. At the end of 1942 I went back to China alone, taking a Norwegian freighter

18

from New York, sailing south through the Panama Canal, down the west coast of South America, around the Horn, over to Cape Town for a day, then around Africa up to Karachi. There we disembarked, and by great good luck, I reached New Delhi in time to spend Christmas with my aunt, Grace Stockwell, who was refugeeing from Burma. After a short time in India, it was "over the Hump" to Chungking, and then on to Chengtu.

Those two war years were both a dream and a nightmare. Even as I recall the facts, it is hard to believe them true. For me they were confined largely to Chengtu and to the campus of the West China Union University. Chengtu is the political capital of Szechwan province, as Chungking is its financial capital, and lies three hundred miles northwest of the latter city. Just outside the wall of this city of nearly six hundred thousand people is the campus of the University. Here about three hundred acres of flat land comprise the University campus, with some ten large college buildings at its center and a row of missionary residences and dormitories around its perimeter. It is the creation of five missions which were persuaded to work together by Joe Beech, its first chancellor. To have welded British, Canadian, and American mission bodies into one educational effort is a testimony to the faith, courage, and mediating genius of Uncle Joe. He wanted buildings of Chinese architectural design; the Chinese wanted foreign design. The result is Chinese roofs on the main buildings and foreign roofs everywhere else. Unfortunately, Dr. Beech never got so far as to put up a water tower in pagoda style as had been done at Yenching University, so there is no running water or modern sewage system. The bucket brigade still crosses the campus each day, carrying out the night soil to fertilize rice fields to feed more coolies to carry out more fertilizer in harmony with the age-old rhythm that is China.

During the war years the campus was host to Nanking University, Cheeloo University, Ginling Woman's College, Yenching University, Peking Union Medical College School of Nursing, and possibly some others. All of these were a part of that heroic trek west, a thrilling story of courage and sacrifice in the face of Japanese aggression that can never be forgotten. Countless numbers of educated and cultured people forsook their homes and their comfortable campuses in Peking, Nanking, and other cities. They chose the dangers of travel by bus and boat in a war-torn China, and the difficulties and uncertainties of overcrowded cities and campuses in free China rather than to live in comfort under a foreign aggressor. They could only carry a minimum of books and scientific equipment with them. But they brought their larger experience and knowledge, plus a victorious spirit, with which to cross-fertilize the older, more conservative civilization of the west. Nanking University professors showed the Szechwan farmers how to preserve their citrus fruits and how to raise more wheat per acre. Ginling Woman's College reached out in concrete service to women and girls in country villages. The higher educational standards of the refugee schools set new goals for the schools of the west. And the churches profited greatly from the fine spirit and guidance of their Christian brothers and sisters who not only had a wider knowledge of the faith but also could speak out of their own personal experience of the sustaining grace of God through long periods of suffering and uncertainty. To fellowship with them in a common task was a rare privilege.

Luther Shao, of the Disciples' Church, took weeks to make the journey by bus from Nanking to Chengtu. Many days were spent in crowded hotels, waiting with wife, small children, and baggage for busses that were long delayed, often broke down, and always were overcrowded. In these times of worry over long delays, sickness, money, and the future he read his Bible with new appreciation and understanding. When he reached the end of the long trek he gathered together the passages which had helped him most, and published them for the use of other Christians.

Newton Chiang, of the Episcopalian fellowship, started out with thousands of other refugees from Nanking on foot. He had nine boys, the youngest a babe in arms. What belongings they had they carried on their backs. After a few miles the novelty of the experience wore off, and the smaller boys began to complain. So Newton organized them into a Boy Scout troop and led them in a marching song. Food and lodging were uncertain and difficult to obtain. But the assurance of God's presence was so real that at night, sometimes sleeping under the open sky, this Christian disciple wrote religious poetry in praise of Him who gave victory to the defeated. Such men, and such experiences, fertilized the Christian life of the west.

In addition to the Christian institutions which settled on the W.C.U.U. campus, there was the United States Air Force. It arrived to set up a hospital unit in the top story of the clinical building. Each organization had brought some foreign personnel, so we got acquainted with friends from other parts of China and from America whom we would never have known otherwise. In 1946 all of these people had departed.

During those war years transportation had been most difficult. Those were the years of the "yellow fish," that is, the illicit passengers on all busses and trucks, a term taken over from the "pigeon cargo" that stole onto the Yangtze steamers. To describe one trip is to set the problem forth in clear light. I went one morning to the bus station with bedding roll and suitcase, hoping to buy a ticket to Suining, a mission station halfway between Chengtu and Chungking on the north road. I waited from seven to ten to get my ticket. I climbed onto the open Dodge ton-and-a-half truck, squeezing into an already packed vehicle.

At eleven the ticket collector arrived and spent an hour prying some twenty reluctant "yellow fish" off the truck. They protested that, though they had no tickets, they had an understanding with the driver. With them off and the number reduced to about thirty, we started. One mile down the road every person who had been taken off the truck was waiting, with a few more for good measure. We stopped and took them all on. Then in agony and torture we bounced along for forty miles, to the town of Kienyang. It being nearly five o'clock, we stopped for the night. Before daylight the next morning I got to the truck to find it so full that there was not even standing room. I mounted the cab top with two other men and rode all day through dust and cold, hanging on for dear life. If the driver had ever driven over fifteen miles an hour, we would have slid off. At nightfall we arrived at the end of the one hundred and fifty mile journey. This was a good trip, not punctuated with long delays over broken springs, blowouts, engine trouble, or any untoward accident as most of them were. After a few such experiences, I accepted the invitation to teach at the Theological College as the call of the Lord, and confined my labors to Chengtu until better times.

One of the delightful surprises of those war years was the arrival of Fritz and Emmie Fisher. I never heard Fritz tell his story, but as I picked up bits here and there, this seems to be the general idea. Fritz was a Jew, educated in

Austria, and Emmie was a Catholic. Fritz finished his medical course at the time Hitler was launching his campaign to make Germany and its neighbors simon-pure Nordic blood. Fritz and Emmie were in love, and the only thing they could do was to flee, first to Italy, and then on to Shanghai. Somewhere en route they got married. At Shanghai the National Christian Council discovered them and offered them a job in the Methodist hospital at Nanchang. So they went to Nanchang. When the Japanese came in and all Americans were immobilized, Fritz being Austrian carried on. But as time went by he got fed up with the Japanese military. One afternoon he and Emmie, carrying their two baby girls, went for their usual walk south of the city and just kept walking. They got a boat and pushed on to Fukien by river and road, and landed at Foochow. When the Japanese threatened that place, the family flew to Chungking and went on to Chengtu. Somewhere along the line, probably at Nanchang, they had fallen in love with the Christian hospitality of the missionaries and Chinese, and had decided to become both Christians and Methodists. A somewhat difficult combination at times, but it does occur. At Chengtu he stepped into the hospital teaching and clinical work and was warmly welcomed by everyone. His good cheer and untiring and uncomplaining service won him many friends. I concluded that he had received so many hard knocks himself that he had learned to be especially sympathetic

24

to those in need. Emmie was a bit nervous—I would have been too if I had gone through all she had—but she was a good neighbor and had the best garden and cleanest lawn on the campus. They finally called it a day and tried to get a permit to enter the United States to become naturalized. But the list of such people was so long that it looked as if they would have to pass that request on to their grandchildren. So they found a friend who had a friend, and by an "order in council" or some such shortcut, they were admitted to Canada, where Fritz has been serving in a big tuberculosis sanatorium. China is not the only place where to know "how to win friends and influence people" pays dividends. A few months before my arrest Fritz wrote me that he hoped I would hurry home to baptize their fourth baby. I had baptized the other three.

Those were the years the United States Air Force came in over the Hump. It was from large fields a short distance from Chengtu that the first B-29's took off to bomb Japan. There were quite a group of smaller fighter fields where men and planes were stationed to protect the larger fields. Chaplains were slow in getting in. So when the call came, I volunteered to help. Each Sunday for a number of months a jeep would arrive at the campus to pick me up, then stop for the Catholic father, and we would go out to hold Sunday services. They were held in the social hall. First, the Catholic priest held mass. Then I would take

over and lead the Protestant boys in worship. Painted on
the walls were a number of "pin-up girls," blown up to life
size. The boys sat with their backs to these pictures. Evidently the one who arranged the seats figured that if the
preacher's religion was not virile enough to front that
hazard, it would not do the boys much good. Later my
good friend, Chaplain Elon Keeler, once a member of my
Sunday School when I was pastor at Lamont, Oklahoma,
showed up and relieved me of this job. We enjoyed having the boys in our home, sitting around popping corn
over the open grate fire in the evenings and talking of
home. They were certainly accommodating and friendly.
One young lady in Chengtu thumbed her way clear to
Calcutta with an air unit, got a permanent and took in a
movie, to return a few days later with neither China nor
India knowing she had been away. The best thing the air
force ever did from my viewpoint was to fly me out to
Calcutta free of charge after two and a half years in
Chengtu. After that, orders came in that they were to
"evacuate" no more "refugees."

The headaches of those war years were mostly financial
ones. Those were caused by the existence of the legalized
racket called "exchange control." Probably no group of
profiteers in history had a smoother setup than the poli-
ticians and bankers of China then had. Their job was all
very simple and sounded quite reasonable. China was
having her financial difficulties, all centering in the war

and inflation. If America and England would agree to a fixed exchange rate on their money and see that all remittances from abroad were cleared through government banks, that would be of great help. They agreed. But China did nothing else to stop inflation. The big boys on the inside did not want to stop inflation. For they had a perfect setup to reap millions. The racket depended on fixed exchange, uncontrolled inflation, and scarcity of goods. The last two would take care of themselves, and they had control over the exchange rate. Everything was legal and foolproof. America not only co-operated but also granted China a big loan and paid it in gold bullion which was flown in over the Hump at a time when war matériel was desperately needed. The bankers then took this gold and sold it to themselves and their friends at one half its true value, thus turning their paper billions into hard money. But when an American flier was caught bringing in a little gold for himself under the seat of his C.N.A.C. plane, he was discharged and sent home. What he had done was not morally wrong, but he had no right to try to horn in on the main racket.

So we saw prices spiral, going up in geometrical proportion. School budgets had to be revised every six weeks and appeals sent out for more money. Dr. C. B. Rappe sat in Chungking, busily sending out relief money by the millions, all of it gifts from American friends and cleared at the fixed exchange. There was no way to be honest.

You either cleared all relief funds through the banks and were honest with China's profiteers, saying nothing about the rotten deal to the donors (for if they knew, their gifts would fall off), or you were honest with the donors, getting a reasonable exchange for their money on the black market, and dishonest with the Chinese government. Either way you were in a hopeless dilemma. No one who had any American currency or checks which would be accepted by the Chinese merchants bothered to clear them at the bank, for the black market paid three to five times as much. The government made occasional gestures to suppress the black market, but they meant nothing. The higher-ups were having too good a time themselves making millions to worry about the hundreds cleared through private channels.

I have no details as to how much money government and semigovernment banks and agencies cleared during those years. It was certainly many millions, pure cream skimmed off and put back into American banks through the Bank of China. All of us knew the amount must be large, though probably not so large when set against the billions poured into the vortex of the European struggle. But never during those years after fixed exchange was established did we get any more than half value for foreign exchange. One thousand dollars in currency was exchanged at Chungking for a three thousand dollar U.S. draft on the Bank of China, and then this thousand in currency was sold on the black market for twice what the three thousand dollar draft would have brought at the bank. So at that time the government was taking five sixths of the value of all money.

Because of this exchange situation anyone who had a way of getting his Chinese money back into U.S. currency could get unbelievable prices for anything he had to sell. One sold a bicycle for fifteen hundred dollars—no, not Chinese dollars, but U.S. hard cash. Another sold a used piano for the same amount. A small piece of land, about one twelfth of an acre, with a value of one hundred dollars in normal times, brought five thousand U.S. An American medical man who came to China at that time to see what could be done to help in a medical way, bought a second-hand Dodge station wagon, with homemade body, drove it for about five thousand miles over bad roads, and when he got back to Chengtu two months later, sold it for enough on the further inflated market to pay for all his expenses in China and his return to the States out of the profit on the deal. The Chinese government set up a special arrangement to help all private individuals for a time by selling bonds at twenty dollars Chinese to one dollar U.S., payable in New York by the Bank of China one year later. This was at a time when you could get one hundred dollars Chinese for an American dollar bill on the black market. So the American soldiers started to sell their gold salaries on the black market for Chinese dollars and to buy five times as much in gold bonds at the bank's fixed rate. All they had to do was to wait a year, and they knew they would not get home that soon anyhow. But they misfigured. This racket was for the Chinese businessman, not for the American army. So orders came down from the top that the boys must desist.

All of this meant continued inflation and economic difficulty for everyone except the few who were on the "inside." Savings melted away. The only way to save any money was to invest it in things as soon as you got it, and then in time of need go out and sell what you had. Thus everyone turned trader, and all interests became secondary to the paramount need of keeping ahead of the inflation cycle. The national morale steadily slumped. Chiang Kai-shek issued his call to national revival in a book entitled *China's Destiny*, and made it required reading for all teachers and public servants. I read one of the first English translations of this book in manuscript form while traveling by bus from Chengtu to Chungking. It was simply a rehash of the theme that all China's troubles had been caused by Western imperialism, and a call to revival by re-establishing the ancient virtues of China and being loyal to the Nationalist party. Not one word about the social and economic problems the Communists were talking about, and no power in it to galvanize China's youth into action. Furthermore, it was so fascist in its tone and so critical of Western powers that Madame Chiang stopped its publication in English. She wanted nothing to spoil the illusion of a democratic China which she was publicizing in America.

As my plane flew on toward Chungking, stopping at Hankow for refueling and regrouping of passengers, I asked the same question that everyone was asking. Would China, now that the war was over and Japan thoroughly defeated, wash her face, pull up her socks, and settle down to put her house in order? And would the United States help her to do it? All of the financial chicanery of the war years was well known at Washington. But China had to be kept in the war at any cost. We did not know then that the island-jumping program and the bombing of Japan would defeat Japan so quickly. Now that it was all over, would we insist that China clean house and return to ways of honest living?

It is easy enough to place the blame on the shoulders of Chiang Kai-shek. But that is too simple and unrealistic. For it was not Chiang alone, but also his family and associates who failed the country. That is the reason I have entitled this chapter, "The Fall of the House of Chiang." His rule was never a democracy. Neither was it a monarchy. It was a family-archy. The story of his rise to power is well known. After evicting the Communists, this young head of a military academy did the smart thing. He married into the Soong family. This gave him the three legs for his tripod of power to rest upon. It gave him a dominant voice in the Kuomintang, the political party that stemmed from Sun Yat-sen. It gave him financial power, allying him with his brother-in-law, H. H. Kung, powerful banker of Shansi and later long-time finance minister of his government. His brother-in-law, T. V. Soong, may have been difficult to get along with at times, but he had the spit and polish to sell the Chiang regime to America. And Chiang already had a good slice of the military power through his position as head of the Whangpoo Military Academy. So political, financial, and military power were his—not his personally, but his family's. He was following in the footsteps of every ruler China has had for several thousand years, building his power on family loyalty, always stronger in China than any other loyalty. His control over China never came through a defeat of his enemies in any real way, but by compromise. The astute and wily Yen Hsi-sang, Shansi warlord, made peace. So did the warlords of Szechwan and Yunnan. He left them in power, just clipping their wings enough so they could not escape from the yard.

Thus when we think of Chiang's regime we must think of more than one man. For a ten-year period, 1927 to 1937, his government had given China an able and honest regime. But the war years had proved so lucrative in their profits to all of the ones in power that they were unwilling to permit Chiang Kai-shek to do anything to threaten either their income or their special privileges. With no real pressure from the United States, he had no way of "putting the heat on."

I kept thinking of these problems as we flew on to Chungking. The great brown plains of Central China, flat and uninteresting, broken only by winding streams or lakes, gave way to mountains and gorges. Flying in such ease and swiftness, it was difficult to imagine the galling labor of peasant farmers who had cut their small fields out of the mountainsides, carrying basket after basket of dirt up steep steps slowly to build their tiny terraces. The swirling cloud banks soon buried us in a world of fog, but even these could not hide the grim fact of China's struggling millions, millions who live on such a narrow economic margin that they would embrace any revolutionary change that promises a new and better life.

Suddenly we were out of the clouds and over Chungking. I craned my neck to see that strange jumble of blackened buildings, separated by winding streets and alleys jammed with rickshas, blue-coated pedestrians, and honking motorcars, and by occasional splotches of debris left from Japanese bombing three years earlier, all hanging precariously on that rocky promontory that separates the Yangtze and the Chialing Rivers. At Chungking I would rejoin my wife and the Knettlers to jeep it to

Chengtu. The plane landed on schedule at the sandspit in the river, I cleared through customs without difficulty, and was with my family within an hour.

A few days later the four of us started with jeep and trailer for Chengtu, three hundred miles over one of the worst roads in the world. This was my initiation into the joys of jeep travel, a recreation that would occupy a good deal of my time over the next three years. He who travels by jeep has no fear of any punishment in the hereafter, for Satan can devise no more horrible form of torture. A speed of more than twenty miles is hazardous, and to push it up to twenty-five is to hear the unanimous protest of all fellow passengers. One hundred and fifty miles in a day is all one can stand. Add to the roughness of the road the fact that there is only one place in the whole trip where you can get any real repair work done, and you understand why a driver must carry full repair kit with him and be ready to turn mechanic on a moment's notice. Each stop calls for full inspection of tires, springs, battery, and ropes holding luggage and gasoline tins. A broken spring cannot be replaced, but some straw sandals tied between spring and axle may save the other leaves of the spring until you arrive home. If the oil pressure gauge line breaks and you lose all your oil, as happened with me once, Chinese cooking oil makes a substitute that will get you home. It both stinks and smokes, but it lubricates. When brake fluid runs out and you have no braking power, just get some Chinese wine and pour into the brake cylinder. Watch your battery, for the constant jar has a tendency to break the battery apart. It will need renewing about every three months. If your clutch plate goes out, as mine did some fifty miles from home, the only thing to do is to telephone in and wait until a truck arrives twenty-four hours later to pull you home.

When Dr. and Mrs. Glenn Frye from Temple Church at Benton Harbor, Michigan, were with us for a few days, I took them to a country station. In climbing a range of hills, the universal joint went out. Getting my tool box, I climbed out and under, and changed the one from the front drive to the rear. They were quite impressed with my mechanical know-how. I was always willing to loan my jeep to any adventurous spirit, and the borrower always seemed happy and relieved to return it to me. The last friend who borrowed it failed to get satisfactory performance in high gear, so put it into low and drove it that way for one hundred and thirty-five miles. It never ran again. The last I heard it was sold to a junk dealer for one hundred dollars.

Those three years, from the fall of 1946 to 1949, we lived at Chengtu. Those last years on the West China University campus held some delightful experiences, in spite of the fact that they were lived against the background of a steadily darkening national picture.

We enjoyed our contacts with the small group of young

people who were teaching in Oberlin-in-China, a Shansi school which was refugeeing in Chengtu. Supported by the students at Oberlin College and underwritten by a good gift of aluminum trust shares, they had two or more young people from Oberlin on their staff all the time, thus keeping their English teaching standard at a high level and maintaining a fine relation with an American college. A number of their Chinese staff, as well as the head of their Board, H. H. Kung, were Oberlin men. Now that the civil war in China is over, this school has gone back to Shansi, where they are probably insisting they never knew H. H. Kung, and regretting they can no longer collect the income from those shares in aluminum, invested in the heart of "imperialistic America."

For several years Syracuse University had the same sort of relationship with West China Union University. Don Flaherty, a red-haired Irishman, was the first representative. He made travel his major interest, chasing off on jaunts to Peking, Foochow, Amoy, Formosa, and the Philippines, getting back each time to give a few weeks of teaching to the University. There his main concern was to drive some English into the heads of a rather dull class, and at the same time to see that the dean's office did not misunderstand his grading marks. It was so easy to think an "F" was just an uncompleted "B." The next representative sent out from Syracuse fell into a manhole en route and had to go into a hospital for major repairs. He finally arrived and put in a year teaching. Then ended a beautiful dream.

Another dream that was good while it lasted was the arrival of a group of Church of the Brethren (or Dunkard) missionaries who had formerly been in Shansi and a brand-new group of young Mennonites from Goshen College in Indiana. We welcomed them all, knowing no heresy but hate and no orthodoxy but love. We were glad to work with them in the same station, as we did with the first group, or turn over a part of our work to them as we did with the second group. We were land poor, anyhow, having as our responsibility parts or all of thirteen counties with a total population of about twenty million, the only church organization in that vast territory being our Methodist church with twenty-five pastors and a few thousand members. Both groups were easy to work with, and it was a delight to know them. Most of the Brethren left before the Communists came in. They had had contacts with the "Reds" in North China and knew what the score was. The Mennonites stayed on, and learned that the game had not changed. Perhaps we should all have followed the example of these wiser Brethren.

Two buildings were erected on the campus of the University during this period. The first was an educational building. It had been started by a gift from the Cadbury Chocolate people in England, but the "H" shaped building had stopped as a "T," lacking one wing. So after the war, Liu Wen-hui, opium king of the Tibetan foothills, offered to increase his store of merit in the Buddhist heaven by putting on this missing wing. Some complained that West China opium and Quaker chocolate would not mix. They talked about "tainted money." But the only "tainted money" the University knew was " 't aint enough," and accepted Liu's offer.

The second building was made possible by a Christian businessman. The story as I got it was about like this. The manager of the American Tobacco Company at Changsha had a large stock of cigarette paper on hand. When the Japanese made a feint at Changsha, his company wired him to sell it. He sold it to himself, gambling against the possibility of the Japanese coming. They did not come that time. So he then moved his paper out of the path of danger, let inflation pile up his profits for him, and sold at a phenomenal price. Being smart, he then bought U.S. dollars at the ten-cents-for-a-dollar rate that fixed exchange made possible. With all of this good luck, he sent a check for half a million Chinese dollars when Dr. Dryden Phelps asked him for a gift for a church for the University campus. Phelps turned this check over to the University to be put into U.S. money, making nearly twenty-five thousand dollars. That would have been enough to build a modest church of Chinese design to seat a hundred and fifty to two hundred people. But Dryden wanted a cathedral. You couldn't expect an old

38

Yale grad and the nephew of one of her most famous teachers, who was himself as full of poetry, art, and idealism as his uncle had been, to talk in lesser terms. He not only wanted green glazed tile and Chinese gardens, but a large sanctuary, social and administrative rooms, and all the rest. A large committee, representing all Christian groups on the campus, agreed that this temple of religion must be no less adequate and impressive than the buildings that had been erected for the sciences and arts. Dryden put his heart and his money into the fulfillment of this long-cherished dream. Missionary and Chinese friends did likewise. The People's Government guaranteed freedom of religious faith. The building was almost completed within a year after "liberation." That it, like many other buildings, has now been "borrowed" to be used for other purposes was not in the plans of its builders.

The great event of this period was the hundredth anniversary of Methodist missions in China, held at Foochow, Fukien. We did not know then that it was not only the first hundred years, but also the last. Esther and I decided to go, for our first term in China had been spent in Foochow. So we packed our suitcases, I bought the tickets, and Esther dusted off her hat. Chinese women do not wear hats any more than the men wear queues, but since we would be in quite a group of foreigners, hats became important again. So we were off by plane to Hankow, and the next day started for Foochow. But when halfway there, the pilot discovered his hydraulic brake fluid was flowing over the floor of the cockpit. That meant no brakes. So he turned back to Nanchang where there was a long landing strip, came down slowly, and skidded to a stop in the rough fields at the far end of the strip. No one was hurt, and we had a chance to see Nanchang before taking off the next day. We spent the afternoon with Dr. Ernest Weiss, going over his hospital. It had been one of the best equipped modern small hospitals in Central China. The Japanese had ripped out all pipes and metal work and left it in a complete mess. Dr. Weiss had been back for more than a year and was working hard to get it in shape again, in spite of shortage of money, inflation, and difficulty of transportation. He had the Dodge panel truck that I had taken out from America and then found too difficult to get to West China. I thought he needed it far more than I did.

We had a great week at Foochow, saw all our old friends, fought our way through the problems of Central Conference, worshiped in the oldest Protestant church in China, visited the graveyard where lie some of our first missionaries, and were entertained graciously by our former colleagues. Like most missionaries in China, they were living on surplus army supplies, which caused one wit to remark that "everything was spick and Spam."

Dr. E. Stanley Jones made his final visit to West China during that period and preached with his usual effectiveness. Like all the rest of us, he was wondering just how the church would make its adjustment under Communism, which by that time seemed imminent. In contrast to the joy of his visit was the tragedy of the plane crash at Hankow in which my old classmate and friend, Bishop Schuyler Garth, and his wife were killed. The Baptist mission lost a young man and his wife, a Canadian missionary lost his wife, and a C.I.M. missionary lost his wife and four children. It was the most grievous single accident in China missionary history. C.I.M. stands for China Inland Mission, the largest single group of missionaries in China, a "faith mission" whose personnel are unexcelled in their consecration and sacrifice.

These postwar years passed with Esther giving full time to teaching piano, helping with the student Christian fellowship on the campus, and directing the choir at the church, plus running the home where we always had two or more guests. Through her music she opened doors into the lives of scores of young people whom she could have known in no other way. Music often overflowed into religion. These students would come to her with all kinds of problems. One young man even asked her to help him propose to a young lady whom he loved but to whom he did not dare pop the question. Esther invited the young lady to tea, did as he had asked, and received a polite refusal. Thus the question was answered without loss of face on either side. We tried to make our home a pleasant oasis where the weary traveler might always find rest—and a cup of tea.

I alternated between teaching at the Theological College and jeeping up and down the road to Chungking, visiting our pastors and trying to keep them supplied with evangelistic materials and funds. The teaching was the more exciting task. To open up the meaning and relevancy of Paul's letters or the parables of Jesus to a group of young men and women who had never thought about them a great deal, to see new ideas take hold and eyes shine with a deeper apprehension of the truth—to do this even across the difficult barriers of another language was to find joy abundant. Added to this was the fun of working with Chinese men and women of consecration and ability in the multiplied activities of the church and, in some measure, channeling the Christian concern of the older churches of the West into the growing fields of China. The major decisions were made by the Chinese leadership. We had outgrown the day when the foreigner dominated the situation. In good humor and frankness we worked together, in city and market town, in school and hospital, and in local church, making those constant adjustments that are part of any growing enterprise—making them in a spirit of mutual toleration, humility, and surrender to God's will. There were plenty of blunders, probably more by the foreigner than by the Chinese. But with laughter and love these could be corrected, and life flowed on. We were busy, but time was running out and the government showed no signs of reform.

The same old game of fixed exchange and uncontrolled inflation, encouraged by artificial bottlenecks in customs at Shanghai, continued. The postwar years were even better than the war years for the large-scale grafters who were in charge of the government. There were immense supplies of war matériel that they got for a song. There were relief supplies pouring into Shanghai and these developed leaks. There were loans from the United States Congress. The government banned the import of private cars, but brought in all it wanted under semigovernment agencies. It banned the import of medicines, but could not stop the smuggling in of large quantities of drugs from Hong Kong. It put controls on the banks which two British banks in Chungking could not meet, but did not enforce them on the Chinese banks. Foreign businessmen were penalized on every hand as if they were the enemies of China.

Corruption, which is the twin sister of inflation, flourished. T. G. Ho, financial adviser to the Central Bank at Chungking, told the Rotary Club quite frankly one noon that the inflation and economic collapse were entirely due to the bankers who were more concerned about making their millions than in putting China on her feet. Bishop W. Y. Chen and his wife came to Chengtu for a visit. We were invited with them to the home of the provincial Minister of Education. At the feast the latter said that his salary was not as large as that of a teacher at the University. He probably spoke truly. Yet the feast we had that evening cost as much as a month's salary. The answer was that he was getting his salary from "other sources." A few months later I went with the representative of the American Consulate to a similar feast at the governor's home. The same thing occurred. Everyone recognized the signs, and was sure the end could not be far off. Secret arrests of students were balanced by subsidies to students to keep them in school and at their studies. Trouble would cut off subsidies. Yet the cost of living rose so rapidly that no subsidies were more than a pittance in their buying power.

The United States government sent out repeated commissions, and their reports were so discouraging that the State Department did not dare release them. Probably Secretary Dean Acheson saw the picture in its true light and wanted to insist on no more help to China unless she cleaned house. But already the small cloud that had risen at Yenan some years earlier, of which Edgar Snow had written in his *Red Star Over China,* had developed into a major storm. It would take a strong dike to stand against the coming flood. Congressman Walter Judd and Senator William Knowland and their friends raised the "Red scare." They argued that no help to China or any attempt at discipline would mean Chiang's defeat. So

THE FALL OF THE HOUSE OF CHIANG

they voted down Acheson's proposals, and sent more help. It was like a father's trying to discipline his wayward son, while his mother gives him all the money he wants to spend. The more money Congress voted, the more profits and graft, and the more certain the victory of the Red Star forces.

No doubt Chiang made his military blunders. The long and costly holding of Mukden could not be defended in terms of military strategy. One newspaper correspondent who had been on the inside for months told me that Chiang did not trust his generals. His men would work out a plan of defense or attack, then Chiang would fly into the situation at the last moment, order a complete change of plan according to his ideas, and not only lose the battles but also take the heart out of his responsible subordinates.

But whether this be true or not, no strategist in the world can fight a successful war when the very ones upon whom he must depend to finance and equip his army are working at cross-purposes. The battles were not lost at the front, but in Nanking and commercial centers where the money-changers were salting away their millions in American banks. Communism has never won in any country where there was economic stability and honest government. Chiang struck out on three counts—no political democracy, uncontrolled inflation, and corruption in government. China could have forgiven the first, but could not stand the strain of the other two. Whether this shell game is still going on in Formosa, I do not know. But if there is a fixed exchange completely out of line with real prices, you can know it is. And you can know that if it is, the much smaller house of Chiang that is standing there will fall in the same way it did in China proper. But perhaps the members of Chiang's household have learned their lesson, and now know that they have to make their choice between private profit and public good. They cannot have both.

2

Chungking Is Liberated

Looking back over the latter part of that period between 1946 and 1949, it would seem that we ought to have known then that the fall of the house of Chiang was both inevitable and imminent. There were enough straws blown by the wind to let us know that a major storm was fast approaching. In the spring of 1947 several truck-loads of missionaries from Sian belonging to the Scandinavian Missionary Alliance arrived in Chengtu, fleeing from the Communists, and stayed for some months. They reported that the situation was bad. Two English Baptist families came in from Shensi province, and settled down to work on the campus. Two small Mennonite groups came from the north. All the movement of missionary population was out toward the coast. A few months before liberation, most of these folks who had no permanent work in or near Chengtu, came on home, but the rest of us stayed.

Even the United States government seemed undecided. The Consulate sent us advice to get out fully six months before "liberation," but at the same time the J.C.R.R. came in and talked of staying a year or more. A representative of the U.S. Embassy, Mr. Robert Strong, came to Chungking and talked of renting a house. He evidently thought the end far away. So did we.

The J.C.R.R. was one of those apples from the alphabet tree that Roosevelt planted twenty years ago and which a faithful Congress had watered and fertilized over the years with taxpayers' money. The initials stand for Joint Committee of Rural Reconstruction, being jointly American and Chinese. When translated into Chinese, the "joint" was changed to "Chinese" so that it would look to their compatriots as if China were doing it all. Having failed to stop the Reds with direct relief or army supplies, the U.S. was now going to do it by reconstructing the farmer. It was like a bachelor at seventy-five deciding to get married and raise a family of twelve children. A good idea, but a little late. But still—there was no telling what American speed and efficiency might do. So the U.S. flew a million dollars' worth of medical supplies into Chungking and had them nicely stored for the Communists when they arrived. Offices were set up and reams of paper plans were perfected at Chengtu. A number of mechanical sugar presses were built up to press out sugar cane much faster and cheaper than the old Chinese stone rollers. Miss Alice Weed, a missionary with a rare combination of starry-eyed enthusiasm and mechanical know-how, got two of these presses and turned them over to her farmer friends. They lasted several days and then broke. The plans were all right, but there had been no American steel to go with them.

"Jimmy" Yen was on that rural reconstruction committee, placed there by wise boys at Washington who wanted to make sure that some of the money voted got into rural reconstruction, and not all of it into the pockets of the grafters. They knew they could trust Dr. James Y. T. Yen, who had proved by his lifetime of selfless service to the farmers that he really had a concern for changing the farmers' lot. The Japanese had driven him out of North China where he was doing a good piece of mass education work. He came west, and set up a small college near Chungking to train rural leaders. We have had both Dr. and Mrs. Yen in our home, and Esther taught piano to one of their boys. Mrs. Yen visited us in Chungking just before she and her husband flew out to go to the States. One of their sons was an enthusiastic and able leader in the Communist government in the north, and felt his dad was a traitor to the true interests of China by serving with the Chiang regime. Even so civil war cuts across family lines and brings heartache to all.

The storm was moving south. The advancing troops of the People's Liberation Army, as the Communist Army was called, swept all before them. After Nanking it was but a short time until Canton fell, and then they turned toward West China.

I have no "inside dope" on why the Communist cause succeeded so rapidly and completely in China. All I can do is to summarize the situation as I have taken it from books and talks with friends. My guess is that the reasons for its success were four, in the order of their importance: propaganda, honest government, a real army, and Russian help. They had developed the methods of propaganda early in their career. They went to the people in villages and countryside, persuading them through song, dance, and speeches that they did not have to continue to live in a feudal and unjust society, oppressed by landlord and loan shark. They won the people to their standard. Their officials in the territory they controlled lived simply and worked hard, stopping inflation and administering justice with an even hand. Their troops were well led, had been indoctrinated until they knew what they were fighting for, and were well fed and well disciplined. Moreover, their troops treated the common people fairly and won more converts to the Communist program. The troops against which they were fighting were poorly fed, poorly clothed, and had no heart to fight for a cause they did not understand. The Russians turned over to them the captured Japanese supplies, but probably not without plenty of guarantees that the new People's Government would work in close co-operation with Moscow, especially in all foreign policy. Then the Americans contributed their bit. They equipped Chiang's army, only to see unit after unit surrender themselves and their supplies to the Reds. By the time the Communists were halfway across China they could throw away all old Japanese war matériel. There was plenty of better American equipment at hand. When they got to Chungking, not one truck in twenty came from Russia or anywhere else but good old Uncle Sam. The U.S.A. did all it could to forward the Communist program. But this is to get ahead of my story.

We did not move to Chungking to help prepare the welcome party for the victorious troops who arrived three months later. We went down because Dr. and Mrs. C. B. Rappe were going home, and there was no one else to step into the situation. Bert and Grace Rappe had spent their lives in Chungking. They had countless friends. Bert said that he had never offended a Chinese, which I think was true, but, from the standpoint of administrative responsibilities, not always too wise. No one ever gave himself more selflessly to the Chinese than Dr. C. B. Rappe. During the war, he was in Chungking while his wife was in the States. When the Central Government moved up to its wartime capital, a score of government and relief agencies moved to the campus of the Methodist High School, and Bert found a place for them all. As a host, whether to Chinese or foreign guests, he was gracious and helpful. He ran a bachelor's mess during the war years, and too many of us have sat at his table ever to forget his kindly hospitality. He was unswervingly loyal to the Central Government and avoided the black market as he would the bubonic plague. He handled millions of dollars of relief funds and mission money and did it efficiently and without sputtering or fuss. Bert worked for and with the Chinese, and he would be sorely missed. The Chinese never forget a friend who has done them a personal favor. The political favor of taking Japan off their backs was different.

So I went down to Chungking in May to take over the treasurer's books and to help Dr. and Mrs. Rappe get packed and away. Mrs. Rappe had to have medical attention without delay, so they would go out by air, with one or two steamer trunks and suitcases. In the usual way, they were gracious in leaving the house furnished, even curtains on the windows and the cook in the kitchen. We were to move down in the fall and would need both. As Mrs. Rappe was leaving, her parting remark was, "Olin, I tremble to think of all the problems we are leaving you." If she had known these problems would put me in jail for nearly two years, she would not only have trembled; she would have had an ague.

The summer of 1949 was spent commuting between Chengtu and Chungking, trying to cover the responsibilities at both places, and hauling silver dollars up and down the road. Remittances through the banks were almost useless. The banks could not keep up with the inflation cycle and delayed for days in making payments on the drafts received. Silver came in again, and the missions ganged together at Chengtu so that in selling checks to merchants we would not be bidding against one another. Some weeks we had all we wanted; other weeks we starved. In the middle of the summer orders came from Nanking legalizing all the old subsidiary coins, nickles and dimes, which had been worthless for several years. The manager of the Central Bank who received this telegram held it up for twenty-four hours while his underlings went out and bought all they could for next to nothing. There was talk of prosecution, but everyone was too busy to press the matter. I made periodic visits to country stations, taking all the silver dollars I could in my jeep. Since they weigh about thirty pounds to a thousand, I often had a load.

Early in September we moved to Chungking. The Reverend Fred Nelson, a missionary of the Scandinavian group, a man who wears his wings under his soiled mechanic's coveralls, was the saint who trucked piano, trunks, and other things down for us. We drove down in a Ford station wagon that I had acquired, a big step-up from the jeep. We had hardly settled in Chungking until Canton fell and the armies moved west. I made one more hurried trip to Chengtu on mission business, and then put the car away, and battened down the shutters for the storm. By mid-October the United States Consulate was moving out and the end was certain and near.

Then who should appear but the Reverend William Schubert. He came in on one of the last planes from Hong Kong, arriving just a month before the Communists did. He had been home on furlough, and since the Methodist Board did not think it wise that he go back, he had just jumped a plane and came anyway. He said it was "the Lord's leading." Evidently the Board got no such information from Headquarters and fired him for insubordination. But he said that firing did not matter, for he had lots of friends in his native California and the Lord had never forsaken him yet. Will is a great fellow, and while he and I do not speak the same dialect when we get into the field of Biblical interpretation, there is no doubt about his religious sincerity and depth. He was with Esther and me the night I was arrested, and assured me that I did not need to worry; God would take care of me. He certainly told the truth, truth he had learned out of his own experience. He helped in a couple of revivals before the Communists arrived, taught some courses in a Bible school at Chungking, and continued to publish his *Revival News* until the government told him that it must be registered. (They would not register it.)

During that last month we had one other guest, Mr. Spencer Moosa, an Associated Press correspondent. He dropped into my office one day, saying he was looking for a place to stay. The Consulate was full up, so I suggested he stay with us. He was a good guy, quiet and informative on the war situation from day to day. He was the only foreign correspondent in town. He told me that he had had a little trouble with the Communists in Peking, for they did not like foreign newspapermen even as well as they liked missionaries—which meant he was definitely *persona non grata.* I understood that he told the consular people that he saved a lot on his liquor ration while he was with us. He never drank so little in his life. He had escaped from Canton on the last plane, and hoped he would not have as close a shave in getting away from Chungking. He did, however, leaving on one of the last government planes from Chengtu, was there for a week, and then got back to Hong Kong.

The Central Government troops fled before the advancing Reds. Chiang was in Chungking till the end, but he could not get the Szechwan warlords to co-operate in any real resistance. The roads leading to Chengtu were packed with every kind of vehicle that could be requisitioned, and often blocked by those that had broken down. For two or three days we heard trucks moving out day and night. Then silence settled over the city for forty-eight hours. The first night there were terrific blasts caused by blowing up the arsenal a few miles up the river. Windows broke from the concussion. There was a report of thousands killed in and near the explosion, but I had no confirmation of this story.

A short distance out of the city was a prison for political prisoners. It had been established during the war against Japan and was also used as a training center for secret-service men. After the war it was used by Chiang for Communist prisoners. Three days before the Communists arrived, between two and three hundred political prisoners there were shot and burned. This must have been done with the full consent of Chiang Kai-shek, for they were important people and he had not left yet. This fact was reported to me by a fellow missionary who had been out to the place a day or so after "liberation" and had seen the horrible remains. One of his Christian students perished there. Since the U.S. army had helped establish this place in the earlier years, Communist propaganda blamed imperialistic America and Chiang Kai-shek equally for the deed.

The end came quickly and painlessly. One day and night of deathlike silence, with all people in their homes, and with gates and doors barred; then the second morning a salvo of firecrackers, welcoming the incoming troops. There was no fighting, but the troops were weary from long, hard marching. Doors opened, and people thronged out onto the streets. Before long the new flag appeared with its five yellow stars in one corner of a bright red rectangle. We were now under the Red Star, and General-

issimo Chiang was "Bandit Chiang." His stock, along with
that of America, had sunk to an all-time low. A month
later, about Christmas time, Chengtu was "liberated" in
the same manner. The only fighting there was between
two groups of Szechwan warlords, indicative of the kind of
"co-operative effort" that opened the way for the Red
Star advance.

The soldiers who came in were well disciplined and
friendly. They paid for what they got, dressed simply but
well, and were full of praise of their leaders. They were
good propagandists for their cause. After a few days drum
and cymbal corps arrived, and the school campus was
turned into a training center for folk-dance groups and
musical teams. The constant beating of drums drove one
mad. But the Chinese like plenty of noise, and they were
celebrating as well as learning the ways of the new day.

Before long new money arrived. Silver dollars were
declared illegal. Many who had saved their all in silver
were thus without funds. For a few months the side-
walks were crowded with people selling their personal
effects, in order to get money to live. But prices stayed
down, and were pushed down further. The new govern-
mented prohibited all speculation in goods and took stern
measures to stop it. They demanded that every shop make
an inventory of all goods on hand. Then they checked this
inventory a month later to see what had been sold, and
slapped a tax on all held goods. To hold goods and pay

a tax on them did not pay. Prices dropped, and the cost-of-living index which appeared each day in the paper dropped too. Within three months the cost of living had gone down by 25 per cent, the first drop in nearly twenty years. Then to prove they really meant it, the government announced that all who wished to do so could put their money in the bank at so many living-cost points, and when they drew it out, it would be paid, not on the basis of dollars, but on the basis of the same living-cost points. Thus you were guaranteed against inflation. If prices went up, you would get more money; if they went down, you would get less money, but it would buy just as much.

Then the government collected taxes. That was when the first howl went up. For the merchants and landlords had never paid taxes in any real way. Under the Chiang regime, the only people who really paid taxes were the peasant farmers who could not conceal their rice and were too poor to bribe the tax collector. But now the shoe was on the other foot. All landlords had to pay heavily, not in money, but in grain. Most of them had already sold their grain, and so had to go into the market and buy. More than one "ate bitterness" durring those days. They would have been glad to sell or give away their land, but no changes in property ownership were permitted. The merchants paid too, and paid up every quarter, not on the basis of the business their books showed, but upon the estimate of the collector. The collector did not trust the books. If the merchant could not pay, he gave a note against his store and carried on. He could not sell out. He could not close up. He could not leave town. So the government had to sell "liberty bonds" only once to help meet its initial finances. Taxes were sufficient. The people believed inflation was licked.

The attitude of the new government toward those who had been under the former government was very good. There were a few who were shot, but very few. The important people who had stayed were left alone, provided they behaved themselves. All old government clerks and employees were left to carry on their duties. Then as the new government got into smoother running order, many were sent away for training courses so that they might understand the philosophy of and fully co-operate with the new program. All schools were compelled to give major attention to training for the new day, students and teachers alike studying furiously to learn the ways of the new order. Bookshops were crowded and books were cheap. The Communist armies had achieved the revolution, but its permanence was to rest upon information and persuasion. The process of changing the mind-set of China had begun.

Meanwhile, we were all immobilized. We could not travel without a permit and we had to wait. We were first called into the Foreign Affairs office of the police bureau to register for residence certificates. This registry required a detailed filling out of questionnaire, and a question period. By the time they knew all about who we were, where we had come from, how long we had been in Chungking, and what we expected to do, we felt we had earned their permission to stay. This permission was given for six months. When the six months were up, it was not renewed. During the first six months Bishop W. Y. Chen, Esther, and I rented a car and, with the permission of the government, went to Chengtu on mission business. We had a delightful time with former friends, and felt that it was a perfect last visit to the city and campus we had learned to love. Since I could get no permit to drive my station wagon, and all travel outside of town was prohibited, I gave the car to the Methodist hospital to use in their work, either as an ambulance or as a carry-all.

All our guesses as to how the church might prepare for the new day were fruitless. Bishop Chen, eager to help his pastors, had launched a Good-Will Industry at one of the city churches, putting in his own money and encouraging others to do the same. It had run for about six months. When "liberation" was completed, business was so poor for a time that Good-Will could not make ends meet, and the imposition of taxes on it as a business concern finished it off. The orphanage on Yellow Mountain, on the south bank of the river in houses formerly owned by Chiang Kai-shek, had to evacuate and move to a small country center. It still carries on, with a reduced number of children, and has changed its name so that people will forget its former relation to the now "Bandit Chiang." Foreigners found that they were an embarrassment to any church they might be helping, and quietly turned their work over to others. I shifted my responsibilites to Chinese shoulders and prepared to ask for an exit permit. Esther continued to hold her music-appreciation evenings for all who cared to come, and these evenings of listening to victrola records and talking about music continued to be well attended until summer.

But the antireligious propaganda was going full blast, and the antiforeign propaganda stepped up in volume and virulence with the outbreak of the Korean struggle. Most foreigners saw that their usefulness in China was at an end, not so much because they were Christians, but because they were representatives from capitalist nations. I telephoned and wrote our personnel in country stations, advising them to ask for permits and get out as soon as possible.

Not only were the church groups having their problems, but others as well. The Rotary Club and the Masonic Lodge disappeared in the first tidal wave. The Women's International Club tried to find shelter under the Y.W.C.A. tent, but that did not help them for long. The Y.W.C.A. had long been considered so far to the left that many said they had changed their name without altering their initials even before the new government came in. They found it easy to lead the loyalty procession for Christian forces on their march to Peking a few months after "liberation." The local Y.M.C.A. at Chungking went into near bankruptcy and sold off all it could to pay its taxes. The Friends Service Unit which had been in China all through the war, hauling medicines and drugs to hospitals on both sides of the line, was immobilized, and after more than a year of no travel, turned its equipment—trucks and repair shop—over to the Chinese Industrial Co-operatives in the northwest. The fact that it had been purely a service organization did not count in Communist eyes. It had been financed by money from capitalist countries.

One of the minor incidents of the late summer was the slaughter of all of the dogs in the city. The government announced that they were a liability, eating food the people needed, and no longer necessary to guard the homes of the people because all robbery had been stopped. So thousands of men and boys went out with clubs and iron bars and slew all the dogs. Thus Chungking became a dogless city and many a family enjoyed a succulent meat dish. Now if you want to see a dog, you must go to the local zoo where the dog cage is clearly marked, "DOGS, SOCIAL PARASITES FOUND ONLY IN PRIMITIVE OR CAPITALIST SOCIETIES."

During the spring and summer we missionaries held weekly prayer meetings and discussion groups, usually at the Rackhams'. The Reverend and Mrs. George Rackham had started their missionary career some thirty years ago by trying to save the Chinese, and were closing it by saving the missionaries. After the Japanese war was over George had returned to Chungking to take charge of the Canadian Mission Business Agency, which meant that he spent his days in running a hotel for transient guests and trying to get missionaries and their luggage off the river boats, through customs, and on to Chengtu or other stations. After "liberation" he just reversed the process, spending his time meeting planes and busses and getting his missionary colleagues out of the clutches of Communism and back into the friendly arms of imperialistic capitalism. Mrs. Rackham ran the hotel. She believed that a cup of coffee and a little kindly gossip could halve anyone's troubles. The other half could be swept away by a season of prayer or by a hand of bridge, at either of which she was a good partner. To put it in a word, the Rackhams were the Lord's true servants, friendly Marthas of which the church, whether at home or abroad, is always in short supply.

The Reverend Frank Cooley usually led our discussion groups. Even he began to cool off in his enthusiasm for the new government and in his conviction that we could work on if our thinking were right, or rather "left." Frank was another redhead. I don't know why, but as I think over the young crowd, Cooley, Flaherty, Harvey, McCammon—they all were redheads. It looked as if the Boards saw that China was turning red, and therefore decided to send out a harmonizing color. Cooley was Y.M.C.A. man at Chungking University, a man who lived in a simple way with his staff, talked Chinese better than any other missionary around, and gave most of his salary to try to bail out the Chungking Y.M.C.A. Not even Rockefeller's millions could have done that. When the Communists came in Frank settled down to the job of educating his missionary colleagues so that they would be *en rapport* with the new government. He thought the only basic difference between Christianity and Communism was a misunderstanding in terminology. They were really two branches of the same tree. But when the Communists announced that you could not straddle the fence that way, that you had to be all Communist or all Christian, Frank was stumped. For if you put it in those terms, he was all Christian. Then they refused his request to go to Peking. They were not going to have any Christian missionary working among students there. The increase in anti-American propaganda as a result of the Korean struggle finished things for Frank, and he asked for a permit to leave the country. After an unexplained delay of ten months, followed by two months in jail without any trial, he was ordered out of the country and escorted to the Hong Kong border under guard. Thus he finished his re-education in the ways of Communism.

3

Arrest and Imprisonment

The arrest of a missionary was something new in modern Chinese history. It had never been done in the last fifty years. Even when a missionary, some years ago in North China, shot at a thief and by some freak of chance wounded him, the Chinese government never put the man in jail. His own Board was so red-faced over the matter that they dismissed him. But the Communists changed our status for us. They helped to keep "missionary martyr" from becoming a meaningless contradiction in terms.

The first Protestant missionary to be arrested in our part of China was Dr. Marian Manly at Chengtu. Dr. Manly is a unique combination. She can write books, direct plays, make luscious candy, and tell the best jokes culled from her medical magazines. Her job was running a midwifery school to teach the Chinese girls to "catch babies" at the maximum of speed and the minimum of loss. That is a good idea, but ignores the fact that one of China's problems is that of overpopulation. In other words, there are just too many babies. But I love the Chinese babies with their split pants and their runny noses as much as anyone. The ventilated pants are intentional; the noses are just natural. It seems to me that split pants must be awfully cold in the winter. At least when I have rickshawed down the street on a frosty fall morning and have seen a dozen fond papas in front of a dozen shop fronts, squatting on the curb, with their babies cocked up at a forty-five degree angle, saying, "Z-z-z-z-z" or "Sh-sh-sh-sh-sh," depending on what signals were called for, the bottoms looked both cold and red to me.

Dr. Marian Manly had been born in China and had done a great job, but that did not keep her out of the hoosegow when the pinch came. The trouble was that Dr. Manly had a peculiar way of sputtering when she wanted something done, and if sputtering did not get results she took direct action. The picture of "Our Leader"—Mao Tze-tung—hung in the school's small assembly hall. She suggested that it be removed, except when the group was have its patriotic ritual. Failing to get action, she took it down herself. Then there was trouble. Some superpatriot, whom Dr. Manly had probably flunked in her examinations, told the police. Three hours at the police station and apologies both spoken and written seemed to settle the matter. But evidently when she returned to her school she did not wear her sackcloth and ashes in the proper manner. For, about a month later the police arrived one night, marched her off to court where she was properly tried, convicted, and sentenced to five days in the local

jail. She was not charged with being a spy, and therefore
not kept in solitary. She was just tucked in with all the
other women criminals who had cut their husbands'
throats or stolen their husbands' money. When released,
her loyal faculty and students conducted her back to the
campus, protesting that it had all been a mistake. For fear
the same mistake might happen again, she asked for an
exit permit and reluctantly left the land of her birth.

This first arrest really shook the missionary community.
It was quite clear that we were not playing tiddlywinks.
A number who had been on the fence made their decisions and went to the foreign office to ask for permission to
leave. Esther and I had made our decision and on the first
of September asked for the same privilege. We had no
idea how long we would have to wait before getting the
permission.

But we began to pack. That meant boxes, trunks, and
sale of stuff we could not take out. Piano, victrola and
records, and Maytag all went for half price or less. No
private person could buy anything, for he was too poor
or would draw attention to himself if he did. Almost
everything was sold to government organizations, the
broadcasting station, a music school, and such groups.
The clearing of the attic was done on rainy days, as summer heat forbade work there on clear days.

That attic contained the accumulation of thirty years
of castoffs. Most of it was junk. Some of it had collected

during the war years when General Wedemeyer had his air force headquarters on the campus and when both the Reverend C. B. Rappe and the Reverend Harry Haines had acted as voluntary chaplains for the headquarters' staff. There were maps, pictures of the Chiangs, and an army rifle, all of which would have left me red-faced if found by the police. Harry Haines was a New Zealand C.I.M. missionary who married into the Methodist fold without losing either his native accent or complete cock-sureness. He took Dr. Rappe's place at the end of the war, and after we returned to China he went to the States where his wife had preceded him. Two years in the States put a crease in his pants, streamlined his theology, and with American passport in his pocket, sent him back to Malaya, singing, "God Bless America!" instead of "God Save the King!" I have not heard how that outpost of British imperialism that is holding down the fort and hold-ing up the price of rubber has welcomed him. But my guess is that he is doing all right.

During the wait for permits we had visitors from Chengtu and from country stations going through Chung-king, all a part of the grand exodus. One truckload of Canadians and baggage arrived during a celebration in the city, and stayed with us overnight. We were on the outskirts of the city and the roads were blocked by the parades. They had had three days on the road, much of the time spent in inspections. They had only lost some pictures and cameras to the inspectors—no, not as squeeze, but just held because they had no permits. The results were the same, but the idea different.

One day Harvey and his "harem" arrived. Earl Harvey is a tall, laughing-eyed boy from Dallas and good old Southern Methodist University. His "harem" consisted of four single ladies of uncertain age but no uncertain weight. Poor Earl looked like an abstemious, underfed monk beside them. But he had brought them and their baggage through, they sleeping in the truck at night and Earl underneath it, just to keep up appearances. He stayed with us a few days. He did not talk about his fellow missionaries the way I do; raised too far south of the Mason-Dixon line to enjoy gossip. But from a few remarks he dropped, I assumed that he and some of his "harem" did not always see eye to eye. He was a wizard with a harmonica and wanted to teach his young people to folk dance. The ladies protested that dancing was outside a missionary's duty. Earl pointed out that David had danced before the Lord, but they replied that that was in an earlier dispensation. The situation had changed, and now you invited people to prayer and praise. Earl could not see it that way, for he still believed young people liked cake better when it was frosted with fun and frolic. But the whole argument became meaningless after the Communists came in. For then the young people would not come, either to prayer or to folk dance. The American imperialists were their enemies . . . These missionary friends came, stayed a few days, and pushed on. But we continued to wait.

Meanwhile, the national temperature was rising. President Truman had issued his edict freezing the situation in Formosa, promising help to Indo-China, and putting us into the Korean war. The Peking radio insisted that this was all the evil machinations of Truman and Wall Street, and that their comments on America must not be misunderstood as directed against the American "people." My feeling was that by "people" they meant their Communist comrades in the States, who they said now composed a majority of the population. I never felt they had much affection for us missionaries or included us in the "people."

Added to this situation was a local pot that was boiling over, which everyone was afraid to touch. It had a history, and was a part of the Methodist High School. This high school, with its sixty-year history, was headed by one of the alumni, C. H. Yang, a man of ability and considerable influence. He ran the high school as Chiang ran China. It was his private affair. He handled its finances as a missionary I knew kept his accounts. When this missionary went on the district he wore a vest which had four pockets in it. Money from medicine sales went into one, from Bible sales into a second, for Conference expenses into a third, and his personal finances into the fourth. Simple and foolproof! But after a few weeks he got the pockets mixed up, and by the time he got home had no idea how much belonged to whom. So it was with C. H., though he was not handling nickles and dimes, but millions of inflated currency. He put this money out at interest at 30 to 40 per cent per month, and thus could keep ahead of the inflation. His teachers were trying to do the same, so he gave them I.O.U.'s on the rice merchants, which they did not have to cash until they wanted to do so. They would hold these I.O.U.'s until the prices were highest.

All would have gone along all right if it had not been for the Communists. In China they now blame all troubles on the capitalists, but then we blamed the Communists, both those inside and outside the school. Those outside were marching with a victorious army. The farther they marched the more inflation soared, and in the spring of 1949 it went up so fast that all loans at whatever interest rate could not keep up. So C. H. Yang was suddenly confronted with bankruptcy. The Communists inside the school kicked up a big smell and voiced their opposition to C. H.'s educational dictatorship. One part of the school, the Commercial College, forced Yang out and organized their own committee to run their section of the school. Yang tried to borrow, got hold of some funds, and finished out the school year. That summer, with the Chiang government moving to Chungking, C. H. thought he had found a way out. He got the school board together

71

although they had not met for years, and forced the closing of the Commercial College, shipping teachers and students out of town. That would have been all right if Chiang had stayed on top. But Chiang went out. And with the new government coming in, all old scores could be settled. So Yang was pushed out of all the school affairs, a new man put in at the head of the high school, and the Commercial College, with its own head, re-established on the campus.

Then the fun began. The Commercial College had numbers and prestige. They had suffered at the hands of the former regime and its friends. They demanded and collected some two thousand dollars U.S. in blackmail from a frightened Chinese committee, under the guise of school repair money. Then this Chinese committee faded away. C. H. went into retirement. Bishop W. Y. Chen had pressing duties in Shanghai and Fukien. A doctor on the committee moved to Shanghai. Hence, there was no one left but me, and I was the perfect target. I was an American. I had been treasurer of the conference. I refused to pay any more money or turn over any deeds. So I was a foreign spy and was thus denounced on placards, day after day, in front of the college buildings.

Thanksgiving Day, 1950, found us with a half dozen missionary friends in for dinner. Turkey dinner finished our last cans of boned turkey inherited from army supplies. Sunday, the 26th of November, we had the Van

Meters with us for the day. The Reverend and Mrs. Herbert Van Meter belonged to the Oberlin-in-China contingent and were on their way home, having been delayed several weeks in Chengtu by a police raid a few days before they were to leave. They had a small generator next door to their house for use when city lights went off, and it took some time to convince the authorities that this was not a broadcasting device. Herb had been a navy chaplain during the war and had seen active service on Iwojima. He preached and smoked with equal honesty and enthusiasm, and loved his wife and his little curly-headed Dutch daughter, Gretchen, with equal devotion. Gretchen was God's perfect gift to compensate for earlier disappointments.

The Van Meters had just left our house and we were sitting down to supper when the police arrived, six strong, two women and four men. Their leader presented me with a slip of paper which informed me that I was under arrest for mishandling furniture turned over to me by the J.C.R.R. when they folded up just before "liberation," and for disseminating information through the mails. The crew of police then searched the house from top to bottom. They found nothing that would serve their purposes, for the attic was as empty as we could make it, and all books and pictures had been shipped out to Hong Kong by book post several weeks earlier. After the search I took my sleeping bag and air mattress, and the New Testament which

Esther slipped into my pocket, listened to Will Schubert's exhortations to courage, kissed my wife good-by, and went out with the police. A half hour later I was in a small room at the police station, never dreaming I would be there for more than a few days. Little did I know of the way justice moves in new China.

Over the months I lived in eight or ten different rooms in that jail, moved around to meet the exigencies of weather, other prisoners, or building and repair operations. The rooms were all alike, built on the architectural plan of New Jerusalem, cube shaped, and ten feet in each direction. The windows were pasted up with paper so I could not see out, and closed and barred. Smaller windows at the top were opened to let in air and there was an open transom. In the summer I was moved down to a ground floor room where it was not quite so hot. But whether up or down, the summer heat was terrific. I would fan all day, and slosh down topside with a washcloth every half hour. Shorts and shoes were regulation wear. In the winter I often wore everything I owned. On the coldest days, with eight layers of sweaters, shirts, and coats, and with a pair of lined flier's trousers, plus an army blanket wrapped around me, I could get along all right. Chungking fortunately does not get down to freezing, but the damp days make whatever cold there is quite penetrating. None of the jail rooms or offices was heated. In West China everyone just puts on more padded garments in the winter.

My room was equipped with table, stool, cot, and cuspidor. The cot was a flat bamboo shelf, resting on two bamboo sawhorses and easily upset if one got restless. I fell out of bed one night. My air mattress, which held up for ten months and then began to leak, was invaluable. So too the army sleeping bag.

Food was middle-quality Chinese food, the same food that my guards were eating, and I think a cut above what the Chinese prisoners were getting. It was several cuts below what I got at home. Breakfast consisted of a glass of milk, later changed to a bowl of rice gruel, and a slice of bread. Lunch and supper were a large bowl of rice, about a pint and a half, a bowl of soup, and a plate of vegetables and meat. Often a steamed bun, called *mantou,* was substituted for the rice. On the whole, the food was good and adequate. I had dysentery twice, but that is not uncommon in China. The doctor came, and with the aid of sulpha drugs cleared it up. At times I got tired of leeks and onions, for it seemed they appeared every meal. I never developed any great enthusiasm for eels, and ate pig's intestines with considerable reluctance. Sometimes it seemed to me that the pigs had been reduced to liver and intestines only. I was able to buy oranges and candy for a time, but this privilege was later revoked. For most of the year I had no fruit, no candy, and of course no other items in a Western diet. But after the first month I did not mind that, and by the time I had been on

Chinese diet for six months, never thought of foreign food.

Washing, bathing, and laundering were reduced to the minimum. We got one basin of water a day, and usually that was enough. Floor, shirt, and face could be washed with one basin, if you did it in reverse order. To wash a sheet was more difficult, but with hairbrush, table, and soap I could make some change in the shade of color on the sheet. Fortunately, I had olive drab army sheets and the dirt was not too conspicuous.

Our daily routine was breakfast, then trip to the latrine, and exercise for fifteen minutes in the open court. The guards went with us to the latrine to see we did not fall in, then watched us as we were taking our exercise to see we did not fall down, and then saw us back to our rooms, locking the door securely so we would not fall out. They brought meals and hot drinking water, and gave us another conducted tour to the latrine after supper. That completed the day, and our contact with the world.

I have written "our" because there were three of us "foreign spies" in jail at the same time. One was Father Petain, a French Catholic priest who had been helping in a high school. He was arrested on charges of slapping a student, held for three months, and released. I heard him swear that he did not slap any student, but perhaps he wrote a confession of some sort to get out. One of the judges told me later that after he returned to Rome,

Father Petain had written back that he had seen the Pope, told him that he was mistaken in his opposition to the Communists, and that he ought to be a better Christian. Also, he reported that there were three United States secret-service men stationed at the Vatican all of the time to assist in anti-Communist plans. I did not see the letter, but it sounds a bit difficult to believe.

The second comrade was Dr. Stewart Allen. Dr. Allen is a tall, broad-shouldered, blond, blue-eyed Canadian who had been running the best hospital in Chungking for some years. Age, at a guess, is fifty-two. After the "liberation" of Chungking his hospital and mission, the United Church of Canada, paid heavy taxes and kept the hospital going with great difficulty. Dr. Allen had faith in the new regime, and was slow turning all hospital authority over to his Chinese staff. He, like some of the rest of us, had accepted a lot of J.C.R.R. medical supplies just before "liberation," which the new government declared were war loot and belonged to them. But most of all, Dr. Allen had not co-operated fully in permitting his nurses to reduce their hospital working hours for the sake of patriotic activities, and had failed to keep salaries up as high as the nurses wanted. So he came to jail about a month after I did, and stayed there for more than eight months. He was charged with operating on a Chinese patient and then intentionally leaving a dirty swab in the incision so the patient could not get well. The accusation did not make sense to me, but it did not have to make sense to make effective propaganda.

The guards were nice boys. The first group were eight or ten college lads who were just getting started in their Communist training. In the daytime they would look after us, one on the job all of the time, while the rest worked away at the ideas and songs of the new order. At night they would also take turns, looking after us and playing with a revolver which they were taking to pieces and putting together again. I knew if they shot us it would actually be an accident, but I wished they would quit monkeying with the fireworks. Later these boys were shifted to other jobs and a squad of real soldiers from Anhwei province took over. They were just country boys with uniforms on, and were very good to us. When they first arrived, one of them poked his head into the door, said "Hello," and then remarked, "Oh, I see that you are cultivating your spiritual life." That is the term used for a Buddhist monk who goes into a monastery. I assured him that I certainly was. Throughout the whole year there was no threatening, no beating, and no rude behavior toward the prisoners, either Chinese or foreign. We were not treated in a friendly fashion; we were "spies" and "enemies" of the government. But the conduct of the guards and of the judges was decent and civilized in every respect. They called us prisoners their "guests" and, though unwelcome, treated us as guests.

One thing that impressed me more than ever as I lived in prison was the vast chasm that exists between economic standards in China and in America. I had seen that chasm before, of course, but never felt it so sharply. The room that I lived in was standard in size and equipment, all the rooms being the same for prisoner and staff alike. Indeed, we had more room than most, for we were living one man to a ten-foot-square room. The Chinese had two, and sometimes four people in one such room. On the night of arrest, I was wearing my Sunday suit. I wore it all year long, except in the summer. I was the only person around who had a wool suit. Even the chief of police, top man in the whole shebang, wore cotton clothes, and cotton-padded clothes in the winter. My gold wedding ring caused so much comment as an evidence of extravagant wealth that the guards took it away out of sight for the duration. In that four-story building, housing probably a hundred staff, students, and a handful of prisoners, there was no running water above the first floor and no flush toilets or bathing facilities whatsoever. This was in a city where modern sewage system and running water were available to all who cared to pay for them. A series of some ten showers was put in for summer bathing in a small bath house. Otherwise, it was the wash towel and basin of water the year around, with hot water available only for drinking. Nothing was spent on nonessentials. I doubt if any of the guards got more than a dollar or so a month for spending money, and the rest of the staff probably not much more. They watched water and lights with great care, exercising the strictest economy. Communism has not meant any perceptible rise in living standards; it has only abolished the few idle rich. Now all are poor together, and everyone is happier, except the ones who got abolished. In the high schools and colleges fifteen dollars a month is a good teaching salary. Many are living on about one third that much. Such living standards are impossible for Americans to comprehend, but that is where about half the world is living. Of course, I have done even better than my Chinese friends. For I spent less than twenty dollars in two years. But then I was a "star boarder," a Red Star boarder.

The most difficult aspect of the imprisonment was that it was indeterminate and solitary. The indeterminate aspect meant we had no idea when we would be released. One would build up hopes on the merest thread of a pretext, set a date, see that date come and go, with the doors still locked. Disappointment meant an emotional slump. Emotion is a very unstable velocipede. To keep it in control was a major concern, especially during the first six months. Fortunately, I had a pen and the boys bought me notebooks and ink. During the first six months I wrote a total of about five hundred thousand words, spending each day in reading my New Testament, writing devotional talks, articles, a commentary, and letters. If I could find some way to use up six hours on work, I could doodle away six hours, and put the other twelve in in bed. A little difficult to return to childhood habits of twelve hours in bed, but it can be done with practice. The last half of the solitary imprisonment was easier than the first half, and I became increasingly certain that someday the end would come.

The problem of solitary living also became easier. Over the months I had accumulated talks, poems, and articles that I was sure could be used after I got out. I was hopeful that the officials would return to me the thirteen note-books packed with written material which they had taken up for examination at the end of the sixth month. This they never did. Writing was just a part of my "educative" imprisonment. I felt that the educative aspect of it might have been improved upon if I were allowed some reading materials. But aside from my New Testament, *The Music Makers,* an anthology of modern poetry pre-pared by Stanton A. Coblentz, and two novels, I had nothing to read over the months. Needless to say, I got acquainted with my New Testament and the book of poetry. Every attempt to secure Chinese books on the New Order was rebuffed.

Thus the severity of solitary imprisonment, this medie-val thumbscrew seldom used in the West, was made un-necessarily harsh. One day I summed the situation up in these words:

They give you shots for cholera
And typhus from Manchuria,
But there is no cure,
You just have to endure
The pain of claustrophobia.

My experience of prison-sitting leads me to conclude that the three essentials for such vocation are the New Testament, the grace of God, and a sense of humor. The first is discussed in a later chapter. The second, the grace of God, is difficult to describe. But it is the realest thing on earth. By this is meant "God in action." I am not much of a mystic, just a common run-of-the-mill Christian who never expects to get a seat among the saints in the New Jerusalem. The fact that I have been given the degree of M.M. standing for Methodist Martyr, is an accident of fate, not a planned achievement.

But I can assure you that nothing became more real to me in prison than the certainty I was not alone. Day after day when I should have been planning suicide or going crazy with loneliness, I would feel the sustaining power of God. Talks, poetry, and articles flowed from my pen as God led me step by step over those months. What was true of me was true of the others. The Catholic, Father Petain, kept his hours of prayer and song, even though he did not have his prayer book with him, and his pleasant, laughing face each day on the exercise court testified to his inner strength. The same was true of Dr. Stewart

Allen. After they left, a Chinese in the next room tuned up each day with a large repertoire of Christian hymns, spirituals, and arias from *The Messiah*. He was having the same experience and learning the same lessons we had learned, that you cannot isolate a Christian.

The third essential is a sense of humor. Of course you can get along without this third requisite; a lot of people do. But it certainly helps to oil up the machinery and keep the engine from developing a knock. This is one of the subjects upon which I am probably prejudiced. At least, when I remark aloud that if I were a candidate secretary I would be more concerned that young missionaries had a sense of humor than a religious experience, people raise their eyebrows. But the young missionaries can gain a religious experience. Probably their hard knocks will force that into them. But a sense of humor is yours or it is not. Like a tenor voice, you have it in your hormones or you do not. You cannot develop it. By sense of humor I mean more than an ability to see a joke or make a pun. It is that faculty that lends balance to life, enables you to see yourself as you are, and laugh at your own foibles as well as at others', and to recognize that the world will probably keep turning on its axis after you shuffle off. I admit that I am asking a lot. For on the one hand a missionary must have a sense of "mission," or he is not worth a dime. But if he feels he is the "Lord's Anointed" all spelled in capitals, he is a liability to any mission.

83

I never met but one of the real 100 per cent "Lord's Anointed," and never wanted to meet him again. It was on a "President" boat back in 1935. We were on our way to China. This vigorous young apostle ate at the children's table, because at the regular dinner hour people were sociable and some danced. He skipped the captain's dinner for the same reason. A group of new missionaries headed for China ganged up for a discussion group, and asked us to join them. So Esther and I went. That day they had asked a Chinese gentleman who was a returned student to tell them what pitfalls to avoid when they got to China. He made a modest and helpful talk, prefacing his remarks by stating that he was not a Christian, but could tell them what he had observed. No sooner had he sat down than Mr. Lord's Anointed arose and stated in no uncertain terms that he was not going to have any "heathen Chinese" tell him how to do the Lord's work, and stalked out. Amid the awful hush that followed those rude and pagan remarks, I arose, and speaking on behalf of the whole group assured the speaker that the words that had been said represented in no way the attitude or spirit of any of the rest of us. I do not know how long that "headache" stayed on the field, but my guess is that he did not last more than a year or so. Thank goodness there are not many of that stripe abroad. But there are plenty whose quota of humor could be safely increased without danger to themselves or to the "cause." For the Lord loveth not only the cheerful giver; He loves the cheerful—period. And so does everyone else.

During the fourth and fifth months I got to writing limericks. The first were terrible, but they improved with practice. I wrote nearly a hundred of them, describing various aspects of prison life. As limericks they would hardly pass muster. But as a way of giving release to a sorely tried spirit, they were invaluable. If I could see the humorous side of annoyances, laugh at the way the guards always stuck their thumbs into my soup as they delivered it at the door, reflect that I was much like President Truman in that I, too, had a personal guard always with me, and even conclude that my jail room with its light burning day and night was at least like heaven in one respect, that there was "no night there"—to see and chuckle over these things was to keep sane. I fear the Communist officials did not appreciate those limericks. For when they collected my writings at the end of that first six months, they found among them a little booklet of some seventy of these, all neatly entitled "Prison Limericks— Bits of Doggerel Swept Up from the Floor of a Chinese Communist Clink." I agree with those officials. This missionary prisoner was not showing the proper respect for the People's Government. For totalitarianism, when it crushes out freedom, also abolishes that which is just as valuable—the right to laugh.

4

Chinese Justice, 1951

Old China had no law in a Western sense. Social controls rested on four legs. One was the government located at Peking, administering justice through its magistrates and military might. Quite wisely the Chinese observed that the farther you were from Peking or from the magistrate's court, the better off you were. The second leg was the teaching of the sage Confucius. Not everyone could understand what he meant by what he said, but his idea of respect for parents and for the ruling powers had sifted down into the thinking of even the most illiterate. As a moral philosopher he was no slouch. Indeed, he stated the golden rule, inversely, long before it was ever enunciated by the Man of Galilee. He put it in negative form because in the Chinese language the negative form is more emphatic. Thus he said it, and underlined it. The third leg was current maxims and proverbs which were the gospel of the people. They set forth a utilitarian and practical mode of behavior which was accepted by all. To close an argument with a proverb in China is to drive in the final nail and convince everyone that you are right. "Don't sweep the frost off your neighbor's roof nor snow from his doorstep" is the Chinese way of saying "Keep your nose out of other people's business." It's all right to pull your own ox out of the ditch. But if it is your neighbor's, leave it there. You might be accused of planning to steal it. The fourth leg was mutual responsibility. No man lives unto himself, but is responsible to his family and village. This is the key to the myth of Chinese honesty. They are no more naturally honest than anyone else. But the coolies at a mountain summer resort would carry thousands of unlocked baskets and boxes up and down the mountain without the loss of even a baby's rattle because they knew that any theft would be blamed on them all, and all would suffer.

But when foreigners came to do business with China or to live in the Middle Kingdom, they did not understand these four legs of equity. They knew nothing about Confucius, and proverbs were only entertaining aphorisms. They wanted laws that could be understood by all, cleared in a court, and enforced where necessary. So when they had China in a conciliatory mood, they suggested that home-side laws be recognized for foreigners. Since the Chinese government could see no reason for upsetting the whole country just to accommodate a few businessmen and missionaries, it was agreed that foreigners could be tried in their own consular courts under the laws of their own countries, while the rest of China would keep to her ancient and well-tried ways. This arrangement, established about the middle of the last century, was given the horrendous name of "extraterritoriality rights," but in Chinese eyes was known as "unequal treaty rights." Actually, in the eyes of foreigners, they were not unequal, for they were merely guaranteeing foreigners in China the protection of Roman law, just as any Chinese resident abroad had the protection of the same law. But most Chinese were not resident abroad, and this cry of "unequal treaties" was a good rallying cry in every time of antiforeign agitation.

Finally, with the coming of the Republic in 1911, and later with the ascendancy of Chiang Kai-shek, the Western governments agreed that when China had fully instituted the forms of Western law, providing for habeas corpus, trial by jury, and judgment under clearly written constitutional law, the "unequal treaties" might be abrogated and this thorn in the flesh removed. So a large number of students studying abroad concentrated on law. Soochow University, a Methodist school, was only one of a number that made law its major concern. Young lawyers hung out their shingles in China, getting set for a new day. Under the warm enthusiasm and friendship generated by our common struggle against Japan, the final step was taken. The "unequal treaties" became a matter of history. In Chengtu, as in all important cities, foreigners and Chinese gathered at a civic center to hear long and eulogizing speeches, and to drink toasts to the new day in wine or tea, as one might prefer.

The new way might have served the new day if the Communists had not come along and kicked over the soup. But when they came, they threw all legal reforms out of the window. Some non-Communists felt the pages of history had been turned back a hundred years. In relation to the Western countries, they probably had. But the Communists had no interest in Western countries. They were dancing to a tune that came in over the Voice of Moscow. Since Russia is three fourths Asiatic and had found ruling by fist much easier and simpler than ruling by law, China returned to her ancient ways. After all, Saul's armor had proved to be very cumbersome at times. The only ones who mourned—and they did not dare raise their voices— were the young hopefuls in the legal profession. They would have to start all over at the bottom rung of the ladder of success.

This return to the ways of their fathers means that most legal matters are settled in the teashop. When a dispute develops, the wronged party goes to the teashop and airs his grievances. The whole community can know all about them. This habit of washing dirty linen in public does not appeal to us, but the Chinese are not so squeamish. Friends gather around, hear both sides of the debate, then step in to offer a solution. Some kind of a compromise is knocked together, a feast is held, and all is well again.

Just like a couple of lawyers getting together and settling a case amicably before it gets to the court.

The civil court is the teashop in a little different style and with the authority of the government behind it. Here plaintiff and defendant appear, state their cases, and present any proofs they have before a judge who makes the decision, not on the basis of law, but according to his conception of justice. If the case is an important matter, he may postpone decision until he has talked with his fellow judges. From his decision there is no appeal. Thus, justice is administered in civil cases much as in a police court in the States, and with a consequent speed and efficiency that makes the clogging of court dockets impossible. Also, there is no money wasted in lawyers' fees. In cases involving property rights, fees are set for hearing the case. On the whole, this procedure probably makes for as much justice as in the West. The crux of the problem depends on the fairness of the judge's decision, which may obviously be influenced by his own prejudices. Certainly in these days, if you are a foreigner or a landowner, you have the scales weighted against you.

When it comes to criminal procedures, that is another matter. Here I can speak from firsthand experience. For I was a criminal, a "foreign spy."

My arrest was what would have been called a "secret arrest" under the Chiang regime. Now it is the only kind there is. The second night in jail I was ordered to appear

90

before the court. There the chief of police held sway, with two other judges flanking him, and two girls writing down all questions and answers. The questions started, and I discovered that there were many more charges than sending letters to my fellow missionaries in country stations or handling J.C.R.R. furniture.

The court assumed that I was guilty. If not, why should I have been arrested? I sat on a stool in front of the judge's table. He shot question after question. A crowd of soldiers and students stood at the back of the room to see how it was done.

I was accused of being a spy because I had entertained Mr. Spencer Moosa, the Associated Press correspondent, before "liberation." I had accepted mimeograph paper and stencils as a gift from the U.S. Consulate before it closed, so I must have a special relation to the consular service. I had attended a feast given by Chiang Kai-shek and accepted ten thousand silver dollars from him for an orphanage. I had attended the welcome party given Senator William Knowland when he was in Chungking a few days before the Communists came in. I had sent letters giving the world news to missionary friends in country stations. I had accepted J.C.R.R. furniture and helped distribute their medical supplies. I had been listening to the Voice of America, and had possessed a short-wave radio set that was not properly registered. All my affirmations of innocence on most of these charges were greeted with skepticism. Some of the accusations were true, of course, but none of them would have stood for ten minutes before a proper jury. But with anti-American feeling at white heat, and with no law, they were enough to keep me in jail for a long, long time.

This was only the first of such sessions. A short time later, I was hauled out of bed at eleven at night, and made to sit before a judge going over the same questions and answers until five in the morning. Fortunately, I had gone to bed at eight that night, so had had three hours of sleep before the fun began. The results of that all-night session came no nearer to proving me a "spy" than other sessions did. After that the hearings were spaced about six weeks apart, just often enough to let me know I was not forgotten and to build up hopes that someday a decision would be reached and I would be released. To lend variety to the days, a special inquisitor, with a voice like a rasping file, popped into my cell every week or so to accuse me of something that had not come up yet in the trials. He was the one who told me that two of our missionary ladies were also accused of being spies and were being held at one of our country stations for an indefinite period. One of the judges assured me that my imprisonment was not "punitive," but "educative." I wondered what "punitive" imprisonment would be like. It seemed to me an indeterminate and solitary imprisonment had a good deal of punishment in it. But such punishment leaves no marks on the body, only on the soul. His statement resembled one that I read in a speech of Chairman Mao Tze-tung, which was given me during the last lap of my stay in that prison. This statement affirmed that the People's Government was a "democratic" dictatorship because it did not use "coercion, but only persuasion." I decided I would have to buy a new dictionary, for mine had certainly led me astray on the meaning of "coercion."

After each of these sessions with a judge I would get paper and write out a long statement covering the points at issue, giving as exactly as I could all facts that would support my defense, and ways and means of checking the truth of what I said. Evidently these did a lot of good, and the police did the footwork necessary to prove me right or wrong. At least, as the questionings proceeded, I noted that former charges dropped out of the picture and the day finally came when everyone seemed satisfied. But that did not happen until I had been in jail for more than nine months.

The whole of the proceedings could have been cleared and I would have been released or given a fixed sentence within four to six weeks, if there had been any desire to do so. But that is to apply Western ideas of justice. I noted that my two foreign friends, as well as Chinese prisoners, were being treated in the same way. So it was not because we were foreigners. It is just the method that is used under Communism.

My arrest, of course, was partly due to the anti-American feeling at the time. The government used my arrest, along with the arrest of the Catholic father and the Canadian doctor, as proof that they were protecting the people of Chungking from the horrible machinations of capitalists and imperialists. That they could at the same time use our imprisonment as a warning to beware of all wolves who came to China in the sheep's clothing of religion was just their good luck. We were victims of the war situation, not of a specifically antireligious campaign.

But this was only part of the reason for our imprisonment. The major reason for our arrest was that in carrying on our administrative duties, we had incurred the ill-will of some group. There were several score of foreigners in West China, but no one who was free from administrative responsibilities had any serious trouble. Dr. Marian Manly had evidently offended some of her students. Two ladies at Suining were "spies" because they had not been able to turn over to a boys' high school all the money that high school thought they ought to have. The Catholic father was accused by high school students, and since that school was comparatively small and unimportant, was held only three months. A Brethren missionary in Chengtu had refused to yield to the custom of nepotism in the museum of which he was the head, so his staff made trouble. He spent three months in prison. Dr. Stewart Allen had failed to satisfy his hospital staff, and they were an important

94

group. So he was held for eight months in the Chungking jail, and then later for four more months elsewhere. I was under fire because of my connection with the Commercial College, whose head was an important factotum in government circles. So I was held twenty-three months, plus. Later I learned that the government filled the papers with the story of my case, and even issued a special study booklet on it. This material would impress people with the danger of American imperialism and the crimes which Christian missions had been perpetrating in China, and so increase their hate against the American aggressors.

All of this means that China is now following the age-old custom of governing by groups. Everyone is supposed to belong to some social unit, family, clan, village, faculty, labor union, or commercial guild, to which he will lend his strength and which will guarantee his safety. The only "criminals" are those who get crosswise with their groups, or the poor foreigner who has no group to which to belong. In America we would call this kind of government "mob rule," but then we have not studied "the philosophy of the masses." We call such groups in America "mobs" because they are outside the law and employ violence to achieve their ends. In China the ruling group is the law and does not need to use violence.

Thus the ruling group vs. the minorities presents a mixed picture. The only minorities in the country are the Christians—Protestant and Catholic—and the Mohammedans.

These last are concentrated in the northwest and are powerful. Christians are scattered all over the country and are numerically weak. So when the land laws were announced, they did not apply to Mohammedan mosques. They provided for the expropriation of all lands belonging to Christian groups, and to Buddhist and Taoist temples, although leaving all groups in possession and control of their places of worship. The Mohammedans were specifically exempted from any such expropriation. The expropriation of the lands can be defended on the basis of the Communist program, but this evident discrimination cannot be defended on anything other than the basis of expediency.

In the light of the fact that all Western processes of law have been abrogated in China, residence there today of nationals of other nations is an extrahazardous undertaking. They have no guarantee of protection againt any individual or group which wants to create trouble. If the foreigners are teaching in a school or working in a hospital, and assuming no administrative responsibility, they *may* have no trouble. If they are in business, their situation is even more difficult. Recognition by the United States of the present regime would in no way change this fact. Even if there were an American consul in every city in China, he would be helpless to protect his compatriots against any injustice. For there is no law to which he could appeal, no objective standard of right and wrong acknowledged by both Chinese and Westerner. Shortly after the Commu-

nists came in, a citizen of one of the north European
countries which had recognized the People's Government
wrote his ambassador at Peking, asking his assistance in
securing an exit permit. The ambassador took the question
up with the Central Government at Peking, only to receive
the reply that all such questions were handled by local
government authorities and they could do nothing. Thus
recognition meant no advantage to this foreigner living
in China.

Several years ago when Chiang Kai-shek appointed a
new governor for Szechwan, we had an interesting time.
The new governor, Wang Ling-chi, was noted for his
harsh methods with students. When he arrived in Chengtu,
he made a speech at a public meeting in which he said
he was not going to stand for any foolishness from those
"blankety-blank" Communists, whether they were students
or foreigners. I shall not repeat his exact words, for you
would not understand the Chinese cuss words any better
than my wife does. She skipped the chapter entitled "Pro-
fanity" in the language book and has not been able to
understand more than half of any ordinary conversation
since. The "foreigners" whom Wang was talking about
were three men, called "The Three Musketeers," whom
everyone knew. He didn't need to mention their names.
One was a Quaker who was so silent one did not know
whether he was a Communist or not. The second was a
Baptist whose sympathetic nature always favored the

underdog, but whose early religious training queered his Communist enthusiasm so that he sang the songs of the New Order off key. The third was a Canadian who may or may not have been a Communist at heart I had a suspicion that he was just a little smarter than the rest of us and was building his ark before the flood arrived. These last two wrote articles to the *China Weekly Review* after the turnover, telling of the wonderful new democracy on the University campus. They forgot to mention that the representatives of the New Order who sat in on all important meetings wore their sidearms.

But when Governor Wang sounded off in his blunt fashion, the news got down to Nanking. Three ambassadors, British, American, and Canadian, waited on the Minister of Foreign Affairs. The results were quite satisfactory. Wang was told to leave foreign affairs to Nanking. He might stage all the secret arrests of students he wanted to, but to arrest a foreigner in that manner would cause unfavorable comment and make some people ask questions. Unfortunately, when I was arrested there was no such ambassador in China, and even if there had been, he could have done nothing. If "The Three Musketeers" behaved in relation to the present government as they were reported to have done toward the Chiang regime, they would not have lasted five minutes. For there are now no guarantees except that you will get into trouble if you do not have the proper respect for the "powers that be," and sometimes even if you do.

There is no appeal from the decision of the court. In every land injustices occur, either with or without law. At times law is perverted by powerful groups or clever lawyers so that it does not administer justice. But there remains the right of appeal. Thus a Negro in Texas could take the denial of his right to study law at the state university straight to the Supreme Court, and get a ruling against the massed prejudices of the Lone Star State. Or another Negro could secure a ruling opening dining car and Pullman accommodations to his people on Southern railroads in spite of all Jim Crow laws to the contrary. Such things would be impossible in China today, and considered absurd. When injustices occur in our legal proceedings we use a medical term and sadly remark that Lady Justice has had a "miscarriage." But in China it is "normal delivery." For the state exists, not for the protection of the individual, but for the protection of the group. Group rights are determined in the struggle for existence, and any individual has rights only as he is a part of his group. To think otherwise is to be an individualist, an idealist, and a capitalist.

Not only does this viewpoint deny the need of legal safeguards for the protection of the individual, but it also makes hash of our New Testament record. From this view-

point, Stephen is not a martyr with a halo, but a simple
fool who got crosswise with the dominant group. Matthew's account of the trial of Jesus condemns Pilate for
that fatuous gesture of publicly washing his hands, thus
dramatically expressing his servile surrender to the voice
of the mob. From the Communist viewpoint, the New
Testament account should have read: "Whereupon Chairman Pilate proudly raised his hand in assent, and said, 'The
voice of the people has spoken. I congratulate you, Comrades, on reaching a unanimous decision so quickly, and
hereby sentence this man in accordance with your clearly
expressed wishes.' The next day the Jerusalem *Daily News*
gave a front-page detailed report of the incident that had
disturbed the serenity of the Passover preparations, and
congratulated the proconsul on the vigor and dispatch
with which he had handled the matter. Long live the voice
of the people!"

I have tried to paint this picture as I see it, with candor
and without any malice. I have no hatred against those
who put me in prison or kept me there. This is partly because God turned the experience into such a blessing that
I came out singing the Doxology, and partly because I
realize, as one of the judges told me, we are all "victims
of our environment." They are victims of Communism, or
they had better pretend to be if they are going to live in
China. I am a victim of a capitalist environment which

does not make me as sad as they think I ought to be. But in either case, blaming them does not help.

The fact that I got my fingers pinched in the new machinery is of little import. When I am in one of my more unchristian moods, I rather wish that all Communists in the United States—not democratic socialists, but Communists—might have a few months of educative imprisonment and a trial such as I had. Then they would not be talking from theory, but from facts. They could say, "I know, for I have tasted, and it is good." Actually, those who preach violence have no moral right to protest if violence be used against them. But my calmer judgment says that you cannot defend democracy or legal justice by abrogating them, even when dealing with those who would destroy the very roof that affords them protection. In patience and in courage we must continue to strengthen those free institutions for which our fathers fought and died, giving all who appreciate them the right to work with us, and defending them in democratic ways against all who would deny their birthright and ours.

5

I Discover the New Testament

That is a strange title for a chapter from the pen of one who has been a Christian all his life, an ordained preacher for much of it, and a missionary for the last twenty-odd years. It sounds as if I never read my Bible.

The truth is that I was raised in an Oklahoma Methodist parsonage where the Bible never got any dust on it. Each morning after breakfast we had family worship, whether father was home or not. Mother could sing, and my old grandfather would join in with his feeble treble, his eyes shining with unshed tears of joy and the part of his cheeks you could see peeping out above his gray beard aglow with smiling enthusiasm. Family worship was no perfunctory ritual, but a vital part of our home life, and the Bible was read.

After Bible and song, prayer. One rather unorthodox missionary and his family came home from West China some years ago. On the way down river, they had a wait of a day or so at Ichang, staying at the C.I.M. home there. The first morning after breakfast, their host announced they would have family prayers. After song and scripture, they all knelt to pray. Whereupon, to the embarrassment of his parents, their little six-year-old son whispered so that all could hear, "But Dad, what are we doing this for?" If Dickie had been raised as I was, he would not have asked. For we knelt down to pray. My father knelt down to pray when he led church service. When he prayed a holy hush fell on the congregation and they knew God was nigh. As a cub preacher, I followed his example until I heard some of the congregation were troubled about it. Evidently the custom had changed while I was away at college and seminary. So I stood and prayed, hoping God would understand that I meant no offense, but was just trying to satisfy some of my congregation who were more concerned that their preacher have a proper crease in his trousers than power in his prayer. I think the Methodists lost something when they took over the Thirty-nine Articles of Religion and the episcopal form of government from their Anglican forebears, but failed to appropriate the kneeling bench as well. The Anglicans kneel when they pray, but they do it in comfort.

Not only did I learn the stories of the New Testament at home, but I had courses on it in college and seminary. Under the inspired teaching of Rollin Walker at Ohio Wesleyan I learned to appreciate the Bible in a new way and value it above all other books without becoming a bibliolatrist, to see the divine in it without being upset by its human imperfections. In seminary I sat under Frederick C. Eiselen, Doremus Hayes, and Harrison Franklin Rall, and drank deep of the books of Harry Emerson Fosdick and that giant of them all who uniquely combined spiritual piety with social passion, Walter Rauschenbusch. He was the one who wrote *Prayers for the Social Awakening,* a book of which a cabby in New York, shifting his chew of tobacco to the other cheek, remarked to his fare, "Yessir, that's the best damn book of prayers I have ever read."

It has become a popular sport in some circles to pour contempt upon these great exponents of liberalism, condemning them for sprinkling the supporating ulcer of man's sin with the rose water of optimism while they sang "The Kingdom Is Coming." Probably some criticism is justified. A little more pessimism as to the perfectability of man might have been wise. But an overdose of pessimism has a tendency to kill social passion and to leave the patient with little more than a pious hope that God will somehow work out His purposes in the uncertain future. Certain it is that if social justice is not achieved under the blood-stained banner of Christ, it will be attempted under the bright-red banner of Communism. For God will bring punishment upon all oppressors until justice is achieved in one way or another. The text for that sermon is in Amos or Isaiah—"first" Isaiah, not "second." One exponent of the neo-orthodox view remarked to me, "Perhaps Fosdick is a great preacher, but he certainly doesn't know what religion is about." To which I would like to reply that when neo-orthodoxy, with its emphasis on the helplessness of man and the omnipotence of God, sends as many missionaries to foreign fields and as many Christians to the ballot box as liberalism has done, or when it writes hymns as great as Fosdick's "God of Grace and God of Glory" or Frank Mason North's "Where Cross the Crowded Ways of Life"—then we can believe it really has something on the ball.

More than this, I had taught New Testament, had shepherded four classes of theological students through the lush fields of New Testament introduction. I had tried to help them see how Matthew and Luke had copied from Mark, the earliest Gospel, and from some other source that is called "Q"; how each one of the Gospels has its peculiarities, Mark being so strong for miracles that he even reports that Jesus withered a fig tree with his curses; Matthew so sure that Jesus fulfilled Old Testament prophecy with complete exactness that he pictures Jesus riding into Jerusalem on two animals at once; and Luke constantly emphasizing the great sympathy and love that Jesus had for the poor and outcast. I warned them that they could not expect literal accuracy, for not even the inscription above the cross which was written in three languages and nailed up for all to read is reported exactly the same by any two Gospels. Other parts of the New Testament have similar problems. There is no way of harmonizing the account of Paul's actions immediately subsequent to his

conversion on the road to Damascus as he reports them in
Galatians and as Luke relates them in Acts. Even the
three accounts of that conversion, all recorded in the one
book of Acts, vary in important details. Many of Paul's
letters are missing, and some that we have are mixed up,
having parts of three letters in one. And we cannot always
be sure of authorship—I Timothy revealing church problems relating to ordaining bishops and feeding the widows
that must have postdated Paul some twenty or thirty years.
I thought I knew a good deal about the New Testament
and did my best to help these young people not only to
understand its problems but still more to appreciate its
unique value. I wanted them to learn to love it and yet not
be slaves to it; to read it that they might get hold of the
living Christ who shines through the colored glass of its
multiform interpretations.

But still I am going to let this chapter heading stand.
For it was there in prison that I did "discover" the New
Testament in a new and deeper way than I had ever
dreamed possible.

To have had my New Testament with me was surely an
act of God, for I rarely carried a pocket copy, my pockets
always bulging with other things. But on the night of my
arrest, as I was leaving the house, my wife slipped me my
copy of Moffatt's translation of the New Testament. It
was a little copy put out by the Y.M.C.A. for the soldiers
during World War I. I had bought it for a quarter when

at Garrett Biblical Institute nearly thirty years ago, and had used it off and on over the years. It was held together with adhesive tape and was completely dog-eared and disreputable-looking. Probably that was the reason the guards let me keep it. When I tried to get them to buy me a Bible, and when Esther tried to send a Bible in to me, they said that the Bible was not allowed in prison. If I had had my morocco-bound Bible that I used most, they would have taken it away from me. But this little New Testament was too insignificant to matter. It mattered to me, for it was the Word of Life, and sustained my spirits through fourteen long months. Never did such a simple act as giving me that New Testament when I left the house mean so much.

One reason that I "discovered" my New Testament during those months was because I had long hours to read it and nothing else. A Bible teacher in theological college once remarked to a group of us that he had never discovered any way to get his students to read the Bible. They would read books about the Bible, but not the text itself. I can now tell him. Put them in solitary imprisonment for months with nothing else to read. Dr. E. Stanley Jones recommends one day of silence a week at his ashrams as good discipline for the soul. I can now speak with authority on that subject, too, for I had not one day, but more than three hundred and sixty-five. He is right; it is good for the soul, provided you have a New Testament at hand and keep your heart open to the grace of God.

The other reason that I discovered the New Testament in a new way was because I was in a place of suffering, uncertainty, loneliness, and hardship. I discovered that the New Testament was specially written for me and other prison-sitters. It might be given the subtitle, "An Anthology of Christian Literature for Those Who Suffer." That is what it is. Every important book in it, with the exception of John, is woven on the red woof of tragedy and suffering. The ministry of Jesus is thronged with suffering humanity, and he addresses his gospel to those who are hungry, weeping, and despised of man. He fellowships with the taxgatherers and sinners, those who knew they were rejected by society and had not a hope in the world. The church is born in the lap of persecution and hate. All through the letters of Paul and Peter and Hebrews rings the constant challenge to be patient, to have courage, and to love in spite of unjust treatment. The anthology closes with a great vision of the final victory for the redeemed, for those one hundred and forty-four thousand martyrs who have sacrificed their lives in following the Lamb. The fact that the New Testament was written *by* people who were themselves suffering and *for* people who were in difficulty makes it understandable only to those who have a real feeling of need. If life is pleasant for you and you have no hungers you cannot satisfy, you do not need to read the New Testament. For you will not know what it is talking about. But when the winds of ill-fortune begin to blow or when the hand of fate takes you by the scruff of the neck and puts you behind the locked doors of economic collapse, moral failure, sickness, or death, open your New Testament. You will find out what it means then.

I first discovered this tremendous fact when the Beatitudes came to light in a new way. I had read them a thousand times, but never saw just what they meant. "Blessed are the meek, those who mourn, the humble, and those who are hungry for righteousness." This sounds like a queer list of people to be blessed. The Chinese list of three "blesseds" is easier to understand. They say the man is blessed who has much wealth, many children, and long life. We can understand that list and most of us would be willing to trade those blessings for the ones that Jesus is talking about. What *does* Jesus mean? He means that you are blessed when life has beaten you down and you know there is no hope in yourself. You are humble because you have nothing to boast about. You are weeping over your own helplessness or others' needs which you cannot meet. You are suffering such moral collapse that you are hungry for a change. When you are in this situation, God can take hold.

The second group of four "blesseds" amounts to the same thing. They are the people who have gone out in mercy and love and tried to make peace until they have been persecuted for it. They have tried to build a new world with the love of Christ, and like the missionaries in China have been cast out or left bleeding and helpless on the field. They, too, have only one resource—to turn to God. When they do this, God again takes hold. Many Christians in Europe learned this truth in bomb shelters during the war. I learned it in prison. It is at the heart of what the neo-orthodox group have been saying. In this they are dead right. Our experience of God's grace is in direct proportion to our sense of felt need. This is one of the two doors through which God's grace enters our lives.

The other door is that of forgiveness of others. This, too, I discovered in a deeper way in prison. For you hardly start to read your New Testament until you come across the Lord's Prayer, and note that the only petition in that prayer that has a condition attached to it is the one asking that God will forgive us our debts. Then Jesus adds, "If you do not forgive men, your Father will not forgive your trespasses either." That is a categorical condition with no exceptions made. During those first days in prison I had to face that condition. I knew that my imprisonment was really not my fault. It was due to a rotten school situation that had been ignored for years by those who ought to have corrected it. It was due to the hatred and malice of a small group of teachers and students who had black-mailed the church successfully for money and then had failed to get buildings and property by the same method. The Chinese leaders who ought to have been on deck to solve the problems had all disappeared or gone into hiding. It was due to the Korean crisis for which I was in no way responsible. I could have spent the days chewing my fingernails and railing inwardly at all those who had caused my months in jail. But my resentment would not have hurt them and would have turned my days into an endless inner torment. That was a dead-end road. I prayed God to take all hate out of my heart, to put love in, and to reign there Himself. That is just what happened. The two doors of self-surrender and forgiveness were wide open, and in flowed peace, contentment, and joy. This is the gospel truth and can be verified in the experience of anyone, anytime, anywhere.

By the way, why do the hymn writers of the church almost entirely ignore this highest peak of Jesus' teaching? There are plenty of hymns thanking God for His forgiveness; almost none recognizing our obligation to forgive.

But before we get too far away from it, I want to go back to this subject of suffering in the New Testament. As I have indicated, the New Testament is full of it. In the Old Testament we have one book on the subject, the book of Job, written as a protest against the commonly held assumption that suffering was always due to man's sin, that it was God's punishment for sin. Job, who is a right-

eous man, through a long dramatic poem, argues with his
friends that the assumption is not true, and that while he
does not know the reason for his suffering, he is willing to
leave the question unanswered and continue to trust God.
When we come to the New Testament, we do not find
the *why* of suffering answered any more than we do in the
Old Testament. But the New Testament goes far beyond
Job in telling how suffering may be used. Like the scientist who cannot tell just what electricity is, but does know
how to use it, so the writers of the New Testament show
how suffering can be used.

They see it as a way of discipline, one or two writers
even going so far as to say that Jesus himself learned
through all he suffered how to be a more perfect son of
the Father. Indeed, we are to rejoice in difficulties, for the
Father would not discipline us unless we were His children. Suffering is also the way of redeeming the world.
Suffering love can change hearts and win men to a new
fellowship with God. This is not only said in words, but
is expressed most fully and perfectly in the death of Jesus.
He saw that his death had this meaning and that the principle of vicarious suffering was woven into the fabric of
the universe. He not only warned his disciples that he
would carry a cross, but told them they must do the same.
As men do carry a cross they gain a sense of fellowship
with Christ that can come in no other way. First Peter has
a great word on this subject. He writes that as Christians

we should expect to suffer injustice, for that is our "vocation," proving that we are true disciples of Jesus. Therefore, when someone criticizes us or offends us or heaps injustices on our heads, instead of quitting the church or going off into a corner to sulk, we should sing the Doxology. For God is giving us a chance to fellowship with our Master in suffering and prove that we are worthy disciples. If we can rejoice, we shall know the comfort of God, that peace and strength and understanding of which Paul writes in the first chapter of II Corinthians.

In reading the New Testament, as when reading any really great literature, you must exercise your imagination. For instance, there is that story of the conversion of Zacchaeus, the head taxgatherer at the city of Jericho. It is the only instance of the conversion of a rich man recorded in the Gospels. Jesus had found that the love of money was a major reason why men did not find God. To have a good bank account and at the same time to have a sense of helplessness and need is almost as impossible as for a camel to pass through the eye of a needle. That it is possible is a proof of the power of God's grace and love.

Zacchaeus was a short man, and that is the key to this story. He had always been a runt. Kicked around at school because he was smaller than the other boys, laughed at for being a pigmy, he had grown into manhood with a sense of inferiority. People despised him. All right, he would find a way to get even, to compensate for his small stature. He

113

early saw that if you had money, people respected you. He knew that the place to make money and make it fast was in the tax game. But the tax business was a tricky affair. You paid the Romans so much for the right to collect taxes from a certain county or district. If you could collect more than you paid them, you were all right. But if you paid too much, you might lose everything. And you had to bid for this privilege against others.

But Zacchaeus learned his way around. He was quick at figures. He knew just how many goats, how many acres of land, how many olive trees every farmer had. He began to climb, and in a few years he had won his way to wealth and power; he lived in one of the best houses in Jericho and was the head of the whole tax business there. People no longer laughed at him. They came fawning to him for favors and loans. He had power. But he did not have anyone's love. He was a high-class outcast. For one thing he was working for the hated Romans, so he was a traitor to Israel. At the synagogue he was given such a cool welcome that he no longer went there. He was lonely, and ostracized.

Then Jesus came to Jericho. The whole town went out to meet him. Zacchaeus took his stand in the crotch of a sycamore tree which stood beside the road. Adding three feet to his height in this way, he would get a good view of Jesus as he passed by.

Jesus had heard of this sharp, short man from his many

taxgathering friends. They told Jesus of his phenomenal success. Jesus could guess what this success had cost, not only in hard work, but in sacrifice of friends and respect in the town. So he is on the lookout for Zacchaeus. As he comes along and sees this richly clothed man in a tree, he knows this is his man. Turning to him, he says, "Come on down, Zacchaeus, for I have been planning to stay at your house." He looks him straight in the eye, and there is such warmth of friendliness in his tone that Zacchaeus almost falls out of the tree.

All of the Pharisees and scribes who formed the welcome committee and went out to meet this famous prophet and healer from Galilee are offended. They think that Jesus does not know what he is doing, and begin to protest. Whereupon Zacchaeus speaks up, welcomes him to his house, and promises that he will give one half of his goods to the poor and repay fourfold anyone whom he has cheated. Probably it did not happen quite that fast, but it happened. Perhaps Jesus stayed there several days before he had won Zacchaeus over. But the significant thing is that Zacchaeus did change. The change was complete. He had found that there was a better way to compensate for his physical deformity, that love and generosity would not only win him the respect of others, but their friendship as well. Also, it brought a new sense of God into his life, assuring him that he, too, was a son of Abraham. That is the story, a story told in a few lines, told in Luke's Gospel.

It is one of the miracles that we often miss, for we think of miracles in the wrong way.

Speaking of this matter of miracles, did you ever notice those lines in the story of the healing of the paralytic in the second chapter of Mark? It is one of the most graphic incidents in Mark. Four friends bring a paralyzed friend to Jesus. Failing to get into the house because of the crowd, they climb up to the flat roof, tear off a piece of the roof, and let the man down on his pallet right in front of Jesus. I cannot figure out how they did this without dropping dirt on everyone below, but then I only know what happens when they turn the tiles on a Chinese roof. This Hollywood type of entrance startles both Jesus and the crowd, and draws everyone's attention to the man and his need. Jesus looks at him and sees at once that his basic need is not physical, but spiritual. He has lost all faith and hope. When he had first fallen ill with this paralysis, his neighbors told him that it was God's punishment for his sin, that he was getting his just deserts. So he has gradually lost courage, and feels God has turned His face away. Jesus sees this. Looking at him, he says, "Why, man, God loves you. He hasn't forsaken you. God doesn't act in that way. You are troubled about your sins. God forgives those, too, and you are a child of His." Jesus speaks with such confidence and faith that the man believes, and all life suddenly becomes new. He can feel hope and courage and faith returning as a great flood. The clouds are swept away and God's sun shines through. Then some of the religious leaders standing by begin to criticize Jesus for talking in this way. Whereupon Jesus says, "Well, if you can't believe the big miracle of restoring this man's hope and faith, if you are too blind to see this, I'll take him by the hand and send him on his way." Which he does. But he still feels that the healing of the body is a small miracle compared to that performed on the man's spirit.

One of our troubles with miracles is that we define them in the wrong way. Some years ago I ran across a definition that goes something like this: "A miracle is any event in the life of an individual or a group that convinces them that God is alive and active." The event may or may not seem strange to others. It is only an authentic miracle in the New Testament sense if it makes God real to us, and convinces us that He is active in our lives. This kind of miracle can happen to us every day, if we have eyes to see. To this I would add one other general statement; namely, those miracles that are reported in the Bible are essential to our faith only if and as they can be repeated or attested in our own experience. For instance, the resurrection of Jesus is central in our faith only as the living Christ is a regnant power and guiding presence in our daily living.

So the months slipped by with me concentrating on the New Testament each day. It never lost its interest, or failed to "crank my mind," as my Bible teacher used to put

117

it. I wrote out nearly a hundred devotional talks on various texts that interested me. I spent weeks on Paul and John, and saw John in a wholly new light. Then I settled down to write a commentary on the first three Gospels. What I wrote was of no great importance but it sharpened my own insights to put down in writing what I found in that study from day to day. The sum total filled quite a number of notebooks which the prison authorities collected at the end of the sixth month. I hope they got a great deal out of them as they read them through. I pitied the reader, for I had a fine-pointed pen and wrote in very small letters. I worked under the constant apprehension the guards might refuse to buy me more paper. But in that matter they were helpful.

One of the most interesting days I had was when I worked over one of the shortest books in the New Testament, the one-chapter book of Philemon. It is a short letter, but a whole drama is revealed in its pages. Paul writes it, and gives it to a runaway slave by the name of Onesimus to take back to his master, Philemon. In it Paul begs Philemon to take this slave back, for when the slave reached Rome, he had become a Christian and is returning to his master a changed man. Back of this simple letter we see the Roman slave system. Probably Onesimus had been captured when some city had been sacked and burned by the Roman legions. He is sold on the slave market, doomed to spend the rest of his life in slavery. He steals from his

118

master and runs away, to be lost in the dark alleys of Rome. But God finds him out, changes his heart and life through Paul or some other Christian disciple, and then, under the persuasion of Paul, he agrees to return to his former master. What an outline for a movie script! How it ended, we do not know. It is an unfinished drama, the ending depending on the character of Philemon.

But perhaps I had better end this chapter as Luke ends the book of Acts, with Paul in prison. Paul was put there by the Jewish conservatives, railroaded into prison as I was. He found his Roman citizenship an asset; my American citizenship was a liability. But he took his imprisonment in the right way, turning "prisoner of Caesar" into "prisoner of Christ." And when he did this, everything became new. He first accepted his fate as an appointment from God. Probably he would not have said that God sent him to prison. But he believed that God could assist, that there was meaning in his predicament, if he could see it. Fatalism accepts whatever comes, and says that there is no help for it. It sees no meaning or value, but bows under the cruel blows of circumstance, perhaps shouting with Stoical endurance, "My head is bloody but unbowed." That is not Christianity; that is paganism. Christian faith believes that while we do not know the reason why, we can find power and guidance from God to use creatively anything that comes along.

What comes may prove to be the way of discipline, as it

has been for me. God gave my spiritual jalopy a complete overhaul. It took a long time to do it, for it was in bad shape. The postwar years had been hard on it. And repair work in China is much slower than in America, for everything has to be done by hand. I left the repair shop with my tank full of the spirit of God, the tires inflated with prayer pressure, the engine running smoothly in the oil of love, and with even a new Duco polish which Paul calls "the spiritual glow." The old car is still only a four-cylinder Model-T Ford, but it ought to run a good way yet.

Paul also was able to use his prison experience for the advancement of Christ's kingdom. He believed his daily prayer for the churches meant much. He knew that his example of suffering in behalf of his faith gave others courage to do likewise. And he had daily contacts with soldiers and friends who were used of God to forward the Christian cause. Through it all he had the constant sense of God's sustaining power, until he could write the most joyous letter of any we have to the church at Philippi.

I know from my own experience now how Paul could write in this fashion. It is a curious thing, but again and again when the going in prison was toughest, the grace of God was most truly present. I do not know if my imprisonment helped any of our Chinese leaders. But I had a constant assurance that the months spent there would not be wasted, and that in ways far more wonderful than I could guess, the experience would fit into God's great economy for the accomplishment of His purposes. This confidence, fostered both by the sense of His presence and by the teachings of the New Testament which I was discovering day by day, brought peace and joy beyond any I had ever known. That is the reason I believed my years in Chinese Communist prisons may well prove to have been the most wonderful years of my life.

6

Introducing Paul and John

The two greatest figures in the New Testament, aside from the Master, are Paul and "the unknown disciple," John. These two have had a greater influence on the Christian movement, both in their own time and in succeeding centuries, than Peter or any other of the early apostles. Yet both of them were outside that sacred inner circle of official leaders at Jerusalem who were called apostles because they could bear eyewitness testimony to the resurrection of Jesus.

Of both of these men our knowledge is much less than we wish it were. At first reading the record of Paul's life and labors in Acts seems to be quite adequate. It is told with vividness and holds the reader spellbound. But when we turn to the letters of Paul, we find there are large gaps of information which Luke does not fill in. Paul reports that he had been beaten by the Jews five times and three times by the Romans, but Luke reports only one. There are three shipwrecks recorded, but Luke tells us about only one, and that happened long after those three. Paul speaks of three visits to Corinth, but Luke reports only two. He speaks of dangers from rivers and robbers, dangers of town and desert, of being hungry and thirsty, cold and ill-clad, and of fighting with beasts at Ephesus. Almost all of these things are omitted by Luke, and we would know nothing about them unless they had been mentioned in one of Paul's letters. We have only all or parts of some ten letters. He must have written scores more of such letters during his lifetime, all of which are probably now lost beyond recovery. But what we do have confirm Luke's picture of a man driven by a passion for Christ, working and suffering tirelessly to establish the Christian fellowship in city after city, and beating out his theology and faith on the anvil of stern discipline and experience.

During my third month in prison I spent several weeks reading Paul's letters through again and again. He grew upon me. Of all his writing, the eighth chapter of Romans seemed to me the greatest single section, and probably the greatest single chapter in the New Testament. It is difficult to be dogmatic in such a statement when you compare such priceless gems as the fifth chapter of Matthew, the fifteenth of Luke, and the thirteenth of I Corinthians. But for range of spiritual insight and theological statement, the eighth chapter of Romans is probably the peak.

Most people recognize that Paul's greatest contribution to Christianity was his clear emphasis on faith as the one and only condition of salvation. But certainly of equal importance was to see clearly and interpret courageously the meaning of the cross. Some have tried to argue that Paul led Christianity astray from the simple teachings of Jesus. Paul did nothing of the kind. He saved Christianity in a world that would have been glad to alter its fundamental message. For to that world the cross was an odious byword and black shame. Cicero wrote that the very word "cross" was so loathsome no cultured man would admit it to his vocabulary. The sadistic mind of man had never invented a more cruel and hideous death. Yet that was how Christ had died, and to preach a Redeemer who had thus died took insight and courage of a high order.

Peter did not have that courage or insight. The first sermons in Acts emphasize the resurrection, not the suffering love of a redeeming God. Peter even backslid on his vision that he go to the Gentiles, and in spite of the fact that he had baptized the uncircumcised Cornelius and his family, refused to eat with the Gentiles at Antioch. No other apostle did any better than Peter.

But Paul saw the issue and grasped the nettle of the cross in both hands. Holding it up, he cried, "Ashamed of the cross? Never! It is our badge of courage. It is the worst that life can do to anyone. If God can change such a defeat into a victory, then we have no fears. He who raised Christ from the dead will raise us as well, if we suffer with him. Ashamed of the cross? Never! It is our assurance that God loves us. It was not an accident, but within the planned purpose of God, revealing the lengths God is willing to go

124

to destroy the power of sin and win us to His sonship. We have been bought with a price, therefore, glorify God."

Paul drew upon every analogy that he could think of—the Jewish sacrificial system, the slave market, and the law court—to drive his teaching home. No analogy is wholly satisfactory, and when pressed too far breaks down as a complete theory of the atonement. But the one thing that Paul saw was the centrality of the cross, and though it might be "sheer folly to the Gentiles," and a "stumbling block to the Jews," it was both the "power of God and the wisdom of God" to those who were seeking salvation. If Paul had not seen this and lifted it up, Christianity would have become an anemic faith that would never have escaped from its swaddling clothes. It was this courage and insight of Paul that gave courage to Mark and the other Gospel writers to report the crucifixion with candor, not even omitting the scream of agony with which our Saviour died.

Paul did not find everyone happy to listen to his preaching of the cross. Luke reports a signal failure at Athens. Paul had had to take "French leave" from Beroea, going ahead alone to await his companions at Athens. There, since everyone else was talking philosophy and religion, he joined in, preaching "Jesus" and "the resurrection," which the Athenians thought were two new gods. So they invited Paul to introduce his new faith. He did so, drawing upon any points of contact and common experience he could. But when he got to the story of Jesus, his death and resurrection, he lost his crowd. They wanted a philosophy to speculate about, not a faith to live by. They were like the Chinese county magistrate a few years ago who remarked to a group of us, "All religions are good. When I get time, I am going to study them all, including Christianity, because religion is a mighty fine recreation." To such a man, as to the Athenians, a cross makes no sense. For a cross speaks of suffering and can be understood only by those who suffer and have a felt need.

The most amazing thing about Paul is the accuracy with which he expresses the teaching of Jesus. He probably never saw Jesus in the flesh. He does not quote his teaching, except perhaps once. Yet you can take the twelfth chapter of Romans or any of the practical exhortations with which he closes his letters and set them alongside the Sermon on the Mount. The wording is different, but the ideas and spirit are identical.

Paul never fails to ring the bell unless it be in his exhortations to the women to keep silent in church, to keep their heads covered and to obey their husbands. In these matters he reveals his concern for keeping the Christian fellowship from unnecessary criticism and disgrace in a heathen society. I never have found out how some of my conservative missionary lady friends who insist upon a literal obedience to all that is in the Bible get around these commands on keeping silent in church. They would surely put a crimp into evangelistic preaching by our women colleagues. Some of my Mennonite friends wear the veil, a veil that is hardly larger than a postage stamp, and lends a certain dignity to the wearer, and makes it possible for the preacher to count his Mennonite sheep without difficulty. But they do not keep silent in church or act as if they believe that "man is the head of woman." All of which makes them better disciples of Christ, even if it is not fully Pauline.

A great portion of Paul's letters have to do with current church problems. I worked away at these for some days and wrote a long article on "Paul, the Churchman." The problems he faced are not the same as those we face in America today. We have no idol worship, eating of meats sacrificed to idols, or the lack of order at communion service. But we can learn from Paul how to face our problems, which though different in kind are similar in ways of solution. Paul always took a problem and lifted it up so that the light of the Christian gospel could shine on it. To those who were quarreling about rival leaders, he writes that "all belongs to you—Paul, Apollos, Cephas—and you belong to Christ and Christ to God!" To those who were involved in moral turpitude, he writes that they must remember their bodies are temples of the holy spirit. And to those who were troubled with problems of eating meat that had been offered to an idol, thus acquiring the spirit of the idol, he writes that they must obey their consciences and protect the Christian fellowship. They must remember their weaker brothers, brothers who were new in the faith, for they were men "for whom Christ died." This refusal to lay down rules, but to insist upon fundamental principles by which each Christian must determine his own conduct, is in perfect accord with the spirit and teaching of Jesus. These principles are applicable today to all our problems of personal conduct.

For instance, in China today playing cards is becoming increasingly popular among the young people. The new government has forbidden majong, the traditional gambling game of China, but recognizes euchre cards as harmless as Flinch cards were in my youth. So the young people are getting great fun out of "da bridg-ee." A missionary complained to me because one of his pastors was teaching his young people this new and exciting game. He never stopped to realize that in the eyes of these young people it was as harmless as tiddlywinks and much more fun. He was trying to apply a law of his youth, born out of another background, not to apply a principle. That is a thing Paul refrains from doing.

Paul has no social message, no challenge to rebuild the social order, though he lived in a society that needed rebuilding. Slavery was widespread and accepted without criticism. Women had a tough time of it, and children were ill treated. But social reform does not appear in Paul's writings. The major reason for this was probably his expectation that Christ would return to set up his reign within a very short time. If this hope were justified, there was no point in men trying to change their status in life. The married should stay married, the single stay single, and the slaves be patient in waiting for a few more years. Their redemption was near. Only the last letters of Paul, probably written from Rome, indicate that he thought the return of Christ might be postponed beyond his earlier expectations. Added to this hope of an immediate winding up of this world's affairs is the fact that the Christian fellowship was just being born. It had to get its toe hold in the world and learn to sustain itself before it could do much about changing the world. Paul had found the Roman government friendly and helpful. The day of the persecution of the Christian church was still some years ahead, and when it came would call forth the condemnation of Christian writers who would speak of Rome as a "wanton harlot." But to Paul it was God's power on earth, of benefit to the church and worthy of respect.

But with or without direct social teachings, any group that set new standards of honesty, chastity, sobriety, and love became a leaven in the heathen society of that day. Men could not ignore a group that "out-lived, out-thought, and out-died" their contemporaries. Not as a social dynamite, but as an acorn dropped into the crevice of a rock, the Christian church slowly grew, sending down its roots to break the granite surface of that heathen society.

The second great figure of New Testament literature is a man by an unknown name. We call him John, but we know no more about him. He might be just "John Doe." Some have thought that he was John, the disciple of Jesus. This view is difficult, and to my mind, impossible to hold. To write the Greek of the Fourth Gospel seems out of harmony with a fisherman from Galilee. To think in the Greek terminology and philosophy of the Fourth Gospel is still more difficult. But added to this is the strange way he speaks of the opponents of Jesus as the Jews. Only once does he identify Jesus as a Jew, but he speaks of his opponents as Jews some thirty-two times, and as Pharisees some twelve times. Nowhere else in the New Testament do we have the "Jews" set apart in this way. The only way you can explain it is that this Gospel must have been written toward the end of the first century or the beginning of the second, written when the Gentile Christian church had broken away from its Jewish origins, when there was a growing tension between Jew and Gentile, and written by a Gentile who thought of Jesus as having been slain by the Jews. We shall never know the answer to this question of authorship. It is unfortunate that this strong emphasis in the Fourth Gospel on the Jews as opponents of Jesus has added to the anti-Semitic hatred that has been a blot on Christian history.

But I am getting ahead of my story. Let us go back and look at the Four Gospels a minute. The first three are Matthew, Mark, and Luke. In point of origin, Mark should have been the first. But since both Matthew and Luke looked over Mark's shoulder and copied almost all that he had written, like two boys copying from their classmate during an examination, perhaps it is better to have him in the middle. They did not copy the same things, but if we put the three Gospels side by side, we can soon see that almost all of Mark has been copied by one or the other, and at times the copying was done word for word. The other two also copied from one or more other sources, and then each had some of his own materials to add. You can buy a book called the "harmony" of the Gospels where this parallel arrangement is clearly shown, or you can do as I did in prison and in a few hours' time work out your own harmonic outline. "Harmony" is a good word for this, for these three Gospels sing the same tune. For that reason they are called the Synoptic Gospels, or "similar" Gospels. All of this is old stuff to people who have read the Bible a good deal, but is worth repeating.

John is different. This was recognized very early in Christian history when one of the church fathers wrote of John as a "spiritual gospel." But if you would realize how different John is, sit down as I did in prison and read the Four Gospels aloud and slowly. After becoming thoroughly familiar with the Jesus of the Synoptics, the way he talked, his teachings and his attitudes, begin to read John. You feel as if you were in a foreign land. Jesus speaks in a different way. There are no parables. There are no ethical teachings such as are found in the Sermon on the Mount, except an exhortation to humility and love within the Christian fellowship. There are no publicans and sinners. His work is centered in Jerusalem. The order is different, with the cleansing of the temple at the beginning of the ministry. There is no Gethsemane, no bread and wine at the Last Supper, and no challenge to bear a cross.

It was this last fact that struck me most forcefully in prison. I was in a difficult spot, and had turned to my New Testament for help. I found that the Synoptics with their picture of Jesus suffering and their high challenges to courage and cross-bearing exactly met my need. So did Paul, Peter, and Hebrews. But John left me cold. There was nothing there that helped me. I could not explain it, for I had always liked John. When in my senior year at high school in Oklahoma City, I memorized the fourteenth and fifteenth chapters of John on my way to and from school. I learned later of some of the problems of this most simple and yet most perplexing book, but I had retained my appreciation of the book. There it failed me, and I felt cheated.

I remembered what my Bible teachers had said about John. One had talked about the deeper spiritual insights of John and had argued that the details of place and name given in John, oftentimes more detailed than in the Synoptics, proved the writer had specialized knowledge the other writers did not possess. Therefore, it was historically dependable. Another had proposed the theory that the differences between John and the other writers could be accounted for by the fact that John was writing for a Greek audience and that he sifted out of his story all that would offend them. He was "defending the Gospel" against attacks of its critics. This sounded reasonable to me at the time, but did not explain the greater number of historical details we have in John.

In my disappointment with John, I turned to Paul and concentrated on his letters, gaining some of the insights indicated in this chapter. Then I returned to John. For the first time I saw a gleam of light.

I saw how completely John is dependent on Paul for his ideas. He really has only two major ideas. One of these is that Christ is the Son of God. The other is that the believer apprehends this through a mystical, intuitive, emotional experience. To check on my guess, I listed all the ideas of John and the relevant quotations from John's Gospel. Then I went through Paul's letters and listed the same ideas and their relevant verses, and finished by doing the same with the Synoptics. With this chart before me, one part of my guess was clearly proved. John's idea of the disciple living "in the Vine," of complete dependence on Christ through a mystical experience, comes from Paul's frequent "in Christ" or "in the Spirit," or other such expressions. Paul is full of this idea, but it occurs only three or four times in the Synoptics, and then with no striking clearness. The same was true of the emphasis on the deity of Christ. In Paul this is frequently stressed in such phrases as "God, the Father of our Lord Jesus Christ." It appears only once or twice in the Synoptics. There are other ideas, but these two dominate in John.

If John gets his ideas from Paul, where did he get his historical framework? To answer this question, I made another chart of the incidents in John and their corresponding incidents in the Synoptics. With the exception of the wedding at Cana and the visit of the Greeks, I could find a parallel for every other incident in John, and for many sayings. This chart clearly proved that John had taken his historical framework from Luke and Mark, had altered it to suit his purpose, and had produced his Gospel. For the first time I saw what John had done and why he had done it. And I saw why I and many others have their difficulties with John. The basic trouble is that we approach John through the wrong door and think of John's Gospel as the same kind of literature as the other Gospels. It is different from them.

John is not a historian and is not trying to write another "story of Jesus." He knows that Luke and Mark are available to the Christian group, and there is no need to duplicate their work. He assumes that everyone knows them. So he can refer to John's imprisonment and can tell of John's baptizing disciples without giving any word as to how John the Baptist differed from Jesus or why he went to prison.

He is attempting something different from the other Gospel writers. He sees Jesus as the ascendant Son of God. He thinks of him as coming into the world, taking on the habiliments of flesh but never losing his omniscience nor his omnipotence, revealing himself to men as the Son of God, and then returning to God by way of the cross, which is not a horrible instrument of torture, but a means of lifting him up so the whole world can see him. He lives like a king, stands before Pilate like a king, and dies like a king. This is the essential Christ, the real Son of God, which in the other Gospels is more hidden. But if man has the spiritual eye, he can see this Christ in the other Gospels.

So John thinks, and so he writes, not history, but drama. His Gospel is a dramatic dialogue, not a "story of Jesus." He is a superb dramatist, not a historian. If his Gospel had not been called a "gospel" and placed along with the others, we might have seen this. For the door to John is not the Synoptics, but the letters of Paul. He is writing theology in the most interesting and compelling way he knew.

Open John's Gospel with this key, and your problems are solved. You do not look for historical facts about the life of Jesus any more than you would go to *Macbeth* or *The Merchant of Venice* for historical data. You recognize that all changes from the Synoptic picture are made to fit dramatic and teaching purposes. John is not trying to deceive anyone. He is telling us what Jesus means to him and to the world, and is doing it in a dramatic form, a way of teaching that will be remembered long after we forget his letters in which he says the same thing. Thus we have in the New Testament a dramatic dialogue draped over a historical framework borrowed from Luke and Mark. In the Old Testament we have a similar dramatic dialogue on the problem of suffering in the book of Job.

If this thesis seems to take the book of John away from you as history, it gives it back to you as a statement of two of the most fundamental truths in the Christian faith. At least, it did that for me. For now I no longer ask about historical details or am perplexed over the seeming conflicts between his story and the other Gospels. These questions have no meaning if this be drama. Rather I turn my attention to the one question, "What is John trying to say to me about Jesus, his relation to God and his relation to the believer?" In answer to that, he says that the Jesus who walked in Galilee, and whom we see portrayed in the first three Gospels, is the Son of God, and to know Him is to know the Father. He also says that I may know this truth in the deepest sense through the mystical, intuitive experience of abiding in Christ. These two affirmations I clasp with both hands. They are at the center of our Christian faith. The Friends call the experience "the inner light." John Wesley called it the "witness of the Spirit." It is the assurance that He is both able and present, that "the healing of the seamless dress is by our beds of pain; we touch him in life's throng and press, and we are whole again."

7

Memories and Miracles

The first six months had been difficult. The days had crept by, minute by minute, hour by hour. As I have said, my New Testament, notebooks, and pen had kept me busy for much of the time and had provided a creative outlet. I do not know how the Catholic father with nothing at all to read or write or how Dr. Stewart Allen, who had only one or two medical books, filled in their empty hours. Perhaps they filled many of them, as I did, with prayer and with memories of the past. Somehow memory has a peculiar power to enhance the vividness and joy of past experiences. I thought much of my parents and my boyhood in Oklahoma, of college days at Ohio Wesleyan, and of the years in the East.

Father and mother were of pioneering stock. My grandfather had settled in northern Iowa before the Civil War, had broken sod there, and raised a family of four girls and two boys on hard work and the Bible, had borrowed money at the bank to pay the itinerant preacher, had voted for Lincoln, and had fought the liquor traffic, voting the Prohibition ticket as long as he lived. Two of his daughters, imbued with the same pioneer spirit, went to Burma and India to preach the Gospel, and one son, failing in his desire to go to Africa, because of health, chose the next best frontier and went to Oklahoma, then known as the Indian Territory.

Oklahoma was the meeting place of two tides of population, one from the South and the other from the North. The northern stream had so exhausted itself in populating Kansas that it had lost much of its strength by the time it flowed across into Oklahoma, only being able to inundate the Cherokee strip and a few counties to the south. Cotton and the Democrats ruled most of the state. The Methodist Episcopal Church, usually called "the North Methodist," came in with the tide from the North; the Methodist Episcopal Church, South, "South Methodist," swept in from Texas and Arkansas. There was never anything other than a tacit understanding, but the general feeling was that a Mason-Dixon line of denominational rights stretched from the northeast corner of the state to the southwest corner, and that all gentlemen would stay on their respective sides of that line. Oklahoma City and Tulsa were open territory, with no rules.

But one could hardly expect a man who had sacrificed Africa for Oklahoma to recognize any such agreement. He was not going to permit any North Methodist to stray into the fold of any cigar-smoking, rebel pastor if he could help it. Therefore, when appointed superintendent of the East

Oklahoma Mission, we settled down in Muskogee. There he gathered the stray members of his northern flock together, and over nine years labored to plant "the North Methodist" church. At the same time he traveled his district to the north of Muskogee, driving a rangy bay horse and buggy. Those were the days of frontier life so accurately pictured in the musical comedy, *Oklahoma*.

Mother was a true pioneer mother, as keen about the building of the church as father. She had only two major interests, her four boys and the Woman's Foreign Missionary Society. For some reason, she had no time for the Woman's Home Missionary Society, in spite of the fact that each year we received several barrels of old clothes from such societies in the east, which father would use to outfit his score or more of underpaid and hard-working preachers. Mother wanted to save India and Africa, as well as Oklahoma. She engineered scores of bake sales and other rackets whereby money could be painlessly extracted from otherwise reluctant givers. The mite box with its mute reminder of the suffering "heathen" always stood on the sideboard. One of the most painful memories of childhood was the time when three of us boys borrowed from the mite box to increase our spending power at the annual Sunday School picnic. Our sudden affluence was noted by someone and reported to father. The next morning's worship hour held some pointed questions and the parental rebuke convinced us that we did not qualify for financial assistance from the mite box, even though we had acted little better than the "heathen" for whom it was meant.

Mother's interest in missions abroad never waned. I was born at the turn of the century and named Olin after Olin Cady, one of the missionaries in West China. My younger brother, born a little over a year later, was named Spencer Lewis, after another famous missionary of West China. Paraphrasing a verse from the Old Testament, I might say, "In missions was I born, and with missionary zeal did my mother conceive me." You cannot tell me that there is nothing in prenatal influence!

A minor interest that mother had was the fight against alcohol. The only trouble was that it was hard to make this fight real to boys and girls in a Sunday School in a state that was "dry" by federal law, a wise provision protecting the Indians from the evils of firewater. I never saw a saloon until I went to college in Ohio. To make the evils of alcoholism vivid, mother would break an egg before the curious eyes of the children, then pour pure alcohol on it, saying, "You see, the alcohol cooks the egg. That is what it does to a man's stomach." She failed to explain that even the habitual drunkard rarely takes alcohol in such a concentrated form. But this scientific truth probably escaped her notice, in spite of the fact that she held a medical degree, being one of the first women to graduate in medicine in the early 1890's. With her, as with most people, cold facts have little effect on a crusading zeal.

This zeal she carried to the end, leaving little else to her four sons in her will than the exhortation to keep clear "of belief in evolution and to hold to the substitutionary theory of the atonement." Probably she knew little about either, but was convinced they were fundamental matters.

After the years in Muskogee, father was transferred to Alva, a town in the heart of North Methodist territory, where there was neither Democrat nor South Methodist nearer than one hundred miles. Here we worshiped in a church where the great stained-glass window, put into the church in the first decade of this century by the local chapter of the Grand Army of the Republic, held the majestic figure of Abraham Lincoln instead of the Good Shepherd. So we could worship under the eyes of the great liberator on Sunday, and go to a barbershop on Monday to hear some resident remark, "Yessir, this is a white man's town. Not a 'nigger' in town, thank God!" After the union of the "North" and the "South" Methodist churches, a preacher from the former "South" church was sent to Alva. But preaching against that figure of Abe Lincoln just took all the starch out of his Southern soul. He had to be moved.

Whether in Muskogee, Alva, or other places, father always retained a vital interest in farming. In early days we kept two cows and two horses, which provided plenty of work cleaning stables, milking the cows, and delivering milk to keep the four boys at home and out of trouble.

For some years we had prize chickens, father having spent one hundred dollars for three hens and a rooster of prize Rhode Island Red stock. Later he added a Buff Orpington strain, and regularly won the blue ribbons and silver loving cups at the Muskogee State Fair. He purchased a farm which produced nothing but taxes and ill-founded hopes of oil. Finally, with the trading of horse and buggy for a Model-T Ford, farming had to be reluctantly abandoned. But he was always a farmer at heart. If he could have shrugged off "the call of the Lord," he would have forsaken the pulpit for the plow. His ministry came to an early and tragic end in an automobile accident. Mother, with sons grown, and cut off from the direct responsibility for church and world mission that she and father had shared over the years, found life had lost its savor. After a few years she gratefully laid down her load and rejoined her life companion.

It was while I was at high school that I dedicated my life to the church for service on the foreign field. We were living at that time in Alva. The Christian people there may have been limited in their understanding of the relation of their Christian faith to race relations or to economic and political problems, but they had no doubt as to the urgency of preaching Christ both at home and abroad. I remember one flaming evangelist who pointed out that if every Christian would win one other person to Christ every year, thus multiplying the Christian fellowship in geometrical ratio each twelve months, it would only take about twenty-five or thirty years to make every man, woman, and child in the world a Christian disciple. It sounded so simple and convincing that I wondered why more had not been said about this strategy. Of course his figures did not allow for shrinkage through those who backslide, nor did it assume that Christian discipleship is not only a decision, but also a lifetime growth. Such preaching, and the slogan, "The world for Christ in this generation," stirred my soul. Under the added inspiration of the annual evangelistic meetings, I set my sail for Christian service abroad. To do that meant a college education and specialized training. For the church demanded both trained mind and consecrated will.

It would hardly be true to say that I selected Ohio Wesleyan as my college. The selecting was done for me. In 1916 father had gone east to the quadrennial General Conference of the Methodist Church in New York, where his one and only speech on the floor of the Conference was an attack upon the tobacco interests and a defense of that provision in the church discipline that denies the Methodist pastor the right to smoke. On his return from Saratoga Springs, he had spent a day at Delaware, Ohio, and a day at Evanston, Illinois, trying to decide whether he would recommend Ohio Wesleyan or Northwestern to me and my older brother. He was willing to lay down his life to build a Methodist college in Oklahoma, but he was not willing to cramp his sons' education by sending them to a school that had not yet climbed out of its swaddling clothes. He chose Ohio Wesleyan. Probably mother's prayers had much to do with the decision, for that college led all others in the number of missionaries it had sent to the foreign field. Neither mother nor father would have dared advise their sons to go into fulltime Christian work. That would have been to interfere with the leading of the Lord. But they would not neglect any opportunity to place us in that environment that would help us to walk in that direction. Unconsciously they, like the Communists, had great faith in environmental influence. Plus the power of prayer! So father took me down to a clothing store and paid out sixty dollars for a blue wool suit of poor quality, the first time I can remember paying so much for so little. Inflation, due to World War I, had hit the clothing market.

My brother and I were "barbs" at college. This was not because either of us felt very strongly upon the subject of democracy in college life or were jealous of the students who ganged together in Greek-letter fraternities. It was simply because we did not have the necessary financial backing to make such a life possible, nor did I have the spit and polish that fitted into such a group. I had never worn a Tuxedo in my life, did not even know how to seat a lady companion at a table, and had been raised in a community where dancing was definitely taboo among the Christian young people. I still remember with what grudging reluctance I paid my share toward the junior-senior banquet expenses when the custom that all men must wear evening clothes to that affair ruled me out. It did not seem quite fair to me that I should be compelled to pay for the good times of others when I could not share in them.

But I did not spend much time grouching about such matters, or envying those who were in better financial circumstances. I was too busy working my way through college. I waited tables at a boarding club, picked apples on Saturdays, and welcomed a six-weeks' all-college "flu vacation" as a gift of God. That gave me six weeks of work tamping ties on the railroad at something more than twenty-five cents an hour. At times life got a bit grim. The first year in college we saw all the other students go home at Christmas. But Oklahoma was too far away, and we needed money. So my brother and I bought bread and jelly at the grocery and ate in our room, thus cutting down on expenditures while we put in long hours at the alumni office earning money by typing letters and addressing envelopes. The only break in this Spartanlike Christmas vacation was Christmas dinner at the home of the Methodist pastor. Packages from home arrived, but not until several days after Chirstmas.

Both of us boys avoided the gymnasium and college sports. We did not have time for them, and every hour spent on such nonessentials lost us an hour at the typewriter and a consequent twenty-five cents. Our study had to be done at night. Themes that were written on a machine always drew higher marks from the English teacher than those written in an illegible scrawl. But since we had only one ancient Underwood between us, we had to stagger our use of it. So the older would study and type until midnight while the younger slept. Then at two or three in the morning I would arise to type my way through to breakfast. Thus by scrimping and working and borrowing we managed to "get through," and to look back upon those years without regret.

The only extracurricular activities that seemed important to me were the Student Volunteer Band and falling in love. To the uninitiated this may sound like a mixture of music and moonlight. But you are mistaken. The Student Volunteer Band was not a musical organization, but a group of Christian students who had volunteered to go to the foreign mission field for service in education, medicine, evangelism, or some other kind of work under the church. I was the president of this Band at Ohio Wesleyan for two years. At that time we had more than seventy-five members. The vice-president was a missionary's daughter from Korea whose sound sense and friendly spirit activated the Band meetings from week to week. Her merry blue eyes persuaded me that I could combine religion and love into one activity, with benefit all around. It really worked out very nicely, ending in a little church service a few days after graduation at which I elected her president and myself vice-president for life.

We were ready to go to the Far East. We wanted to go to Korea, for Esther was born and raised in Seoul and could speak the Korean language as easily as English. But the Board of Missions was suffering from an economic depression which had started for them in 1924 and did not end until the late 1930's. So, failing to get to the foreign field, like my father before me, I chose the next best place and returned to Oklahoma. Five years of preaching and waiting there were rewarded by an appointment to Foochow, China. We looked for the place on the map, found it on the south coast of China halfway between Shanghai and Canton, and wired New York that we would go. Two months later in the summer of 1929 we were on board our ship, with boxes and trunks in the hold, little four-year-old Margaret exploring the mysteries of an ocean liner, a four-month-old baby asleep in a basket, and mother and dad taking turns going to meals or washing out diapers in the cabin.

It is impossible to analyze all of the motives that took us upon our long adventure to the Far East. We always interpret our own actions in the most favorable light. A year after arriving in China, our two children were playing in the yard one day. Miss Edna Jones came along, and seeing the children with dolls and toy beds, asked, "What are you doing, Margaret?" "We're playing hospital," came the reply. "And what is Foster doing?" she persisted. "Oh, he's the doctor." "And you?" "Me?" replied Margaret. "I'm God. I'm helping the doctor out." A big job for a five-year-old, but, like her parents, she was interpreting her task in the highest terms she knew. I was to learn later that the Communists interpreted it in the lowest terms they know, missionary work being nothing more than Western imperialistic aggression carried on under the cloak of religion and all who were involved in it motivated only by greed and by narrow nationalism. Probably the truth lies somewhere between. Western culture could not stay at home. It was on the march, and whatever the motives of those who went to the Far East to share a new way of life and whatever the results might be, it could not be halted. It beat down the doors of Japan, and out of the tensions of the years erected a new and strong nation. It moved into China in much the same way, but created nothing more than a semicolony and a great unrest that was to burst forth in a series of revolutions. The missionary represented one phase of this "cultural aggression." But where others sought to sell cigarettes, motor cars, oil for the lamps of China, and the most modern implements of war, all for the profit of the sellers, the missionary sought to share knowledge, healing, and that spiritual interpretation of life that had been born on a Judaean hillside. The eagerness and appreciation with which Chinese friends accepted, not only the goods of the mer-

148

chants, but also the gifts of the missionaries, and the way in which considerable numbers of Christian disciples labored to make these gifts known and used by others proved that the missionary had not gone in vain. This fellowship in service, a fellowship in which the Chinese took increasing responsibility and leadership, was the most thrilling aspect of our more than twenty years in China.

But I had not only memories that brought joy to many of those lonely hours in prison. I also experienced a miracle. Certainly there was nothing in my situation at the close of the first six months to indicate that a miracle was about to happen. I had hoped that I would be released—not only hoped it, but believed it. Two days before the final day, May 26, the barber came and gave me a shave and a haircut, the first haircut in six months. Then the jailkeeper and one of his aids came in to demand all of the accumulated writing, some thirteen notebooks crammed full of religious materials and a few speeches that were not so religious. I turned it all over with considerable trepidation, not knowing whether I would ever get any of it back. It looked as if the decks were cleared and they would release me the next day. I was so sure of it that I turned my anthology of modern verse and my New Testament over to Dr. Stewart Allen. That left me with a notebook of blank pages and a fountain pen.

The doors did not open. I waited one day, two days,

three days, and then gave up hope. I faced a summer in prison, a summer in one of the world's hottest cities. My room had windows, but they were pasted up so I could not see out and nailed shut so no breeze could get in. Small windows at the top gave some ventilation, but little coolness. The temperature went steadily up and my ten-foot cubicle became a Turkish bath. I sat at my table, fanning myself all day, stripped to a pair of shorts and shoes, with wash basin near so I could wash down my torso every half hour. At night, with almost nothing on and just sleeping on top of sheet and air mattress, I would fan until I fell asleep, to awaken an hour later with sheet wringing wet, covered with perspiration from head to toe.

Then there were the bugs and the boys. I had never had much education in the habits of bedbugs before, had never seen one before I went to China. But I learned fast. I learned that the Chinese name, "stinkbug," is much more accurate than bedbug, for they do not confine them-selves to the bed and always have a terrible odor. I killed thousands of them, and there seemed to be no decrease in their number. If their mobility had been as great as the flea, my situation would have been hopeless. About the middle of the summer, I discovered a way to outwit them. They hate a cold, wet sheet. So I dipped a sheet into water, and spread it, dripping wet, over my cot. Then with air mattress on top of the sheet, I could go to bed with some assurance there would be no hungry visitors before morning. On hot nights the sheet had to be rewet about midnight.

The guards presented a different problem. They had acquired wooden clogs, held on by a strap over the toe. They were cheap and cool. But since every time you put your foot down the heel struck first and then the toe followed with its beat, you got the effect of a tap dancer. To walk up or down stairs produced the sound of a hammer pounding on wood. Changing guards every hour and inspecting the prisoners through the peep hole every half hour involved a good deal of stair-climbing all night long. This did not add to the restfulness of the night.

Heat, sleeplessness, loneliness, no beauty, no books to read, no music—and poor food—are not such as to turn a prisoner into a poet. The food had dropped several notches in quality because it is difficult to get fresh meat and vegetables during the summer. Eels were common, and I learned to eat them without too much difficulty. The guards caught a five-foot snake and had it hanging on the tree in the yard. The next day it was gone, and I assumed it was in our diet. It would be difficult to distinguish it from an eel. I ate everything that came in, had one spell of dysentery, but otherwise came through all right.

For God performed a miracle. He had not opened the doors as He did for Peter, but He changed a lonely and discouraged prisoner into a poet, giving him joy and contentment as he gave to Paul. One could not expect everything, and even God's miracles are limited by the kind of material with which He has to work. God could give an inner fire, but not the wizardry of words. So no matter how I wrote, I was still nothing more than a pinfeather poet, building my insights and ideas into rhymes that might interest some people, but would never make a ripple on the surface of the poetry world.

That made little difference to me. I was having a glorious time. Each morning I would awaken with some line singing itself over and over in my head and impatient to be set down with its fellows. How it happened I do not know. But I never felt a keener sense of God's presence and power, and never before realized that the veil between the physical and the spiritual was so paper-thin. At night I would go to bed with no ideas; the next morning I would have my day's supply waiting. The refilling became so sure that I thanked God the day before for the Christmas present I knew would be on the tree the next morning. The summer passed like a dream. Physical discomfort became unimportant. I was not in jail, but in a garden of poesy. June, July, and August slipped by with a total of one hundred and twenty-eight pieces of verse stored away in my mind and ready to be written down again when I was released. I had had the happiest and most creative summer I had ever known.

Thus God performed His miracle day after day throughout that hot summer. The value of what I wrote was to be found in the spiritual renewal and healing to my own sorely tried mind and heart. Perhaps someday some of it may be of value to others. But this is not a book of poetry, but only a story, and I must resist every temptation to bore my reader with samples of what I did. Enough to say that it centered about the insights that I had had into the New Testament, about the great issues of our Christian faith, and about things Chinese.

8

What Makes Communism Click

When I tell my friends that I spent fourteen months in solitary imprisonment, they gasp with amazement and ask, "But what did you do?" I reply, "I walked the floor until I was too tired to stand, then sat down, and then walked again." But I did more than walk some two thousand miles that first year of solitary life. I thought, not only upon religious matters, but upon political issues as well. I tried to analyze the strength and the dangers of Communism. I had not yet undergone the ordeal of indoctrination during which I saw further into the philosophical basis of Communism and the explanation of why Communists act as they do. I had the impressions gained before I was arrested, what I could see around the prison, and what I learned from my contacts with guards and judges. But these were enough to give me some idea of what makes Communism click.

Now it may be a surprising statement, but I believe the present People's Government in China is the best internal government that China has had for several generations. It is true that I got my fingers pinched in the new machinery. The abrogation of all law seems to me to be a backward step. But it is efficient, and in harmony with the way of dictatorships. When Huey Long ruled Louisiana, or Hitler held sway in Germany, they did a lot of fussing with laws and legislators, compelling them to obey their will. In China it is the same, but much simpler and more direct. You just throw all law out of the window. The name "democratic dictatorship" is confusing. But when you realize that "democratic" really means "paternal"—*for* the people but not *by* the people—you understand.

This new government in China has much to commend it. It is a dictatorship, but all of China's governments, up to and including the Chiang regime, were that. Unlike the others, it is giving honest administration, economizing, and is determined to break the shackles of feudalism and capitalistic exploitation, and take to the people health, education, and economic betterment. Its strength is limited by lack of resources of both money and trained personnel, but its determination and spirit are boundless. One of the wall slogans read, "Our situation may be sad, but our spirits are not sad."

Feudalism has been a running sore in China's social life for centuries. Each community was ruled by its landlords, who together collected high land rents, and high interest rates, and were the backbone of the secret societies which were the unseen but very potent government in the countryside. By dividing up all land among the farmers who till it, and collecting taxes from their former landlords, the new government has broken the power of these landlords and gradually eliminated the secret societies. Along with this, banditry that has cursed the countryside has been stopped. All of this has taken time, and the change will not mean any great lift in economic income. But it is a long step forward.

When they fight against capitalism it is really not capitalism as we think of it in the West. It is bureaucratic capitalism, government officials who turned profiteers and mulcted the people through inflation, high interest rates, and currency changes. During the war, an economist from one of the universities in the eastern part of the United States was in my home. Much to my surprise, he said, "The basic trouble in China's economy is not financial, but religious." He went on to say, "The bankers and businessmen here are not capitalists, but are just money-changers. None of them is willing to invest capital in large enterprises at low interest with the thought of long-time development for the good of China. They are all seeking the highest interest rates on short-time speculative enterprises. If they had a different attitude China would have a chance." It is this kind of "capitalism" of which the Communists are thinking. They are not opposed to a moderate amount of private business that exists for reasonable profit and is trying to serve the real needs of the nation.

The three things that make this Communist government

click are a faith, a method, and a mission. These three, working together, power the new regime in China. I presume the same could be said of Russia.

The faith of Communism is a faith in the determining nature of environment. They believe that a man's character reflects his environment as surely as a chameleon matches the leaf or twig he is on. Change the environment and you change the man. If men are dishonest, it is because there is too much money and too many money-changers in the temple. Sweep them out and honesty will appear. As one of my judges said to me, "We do not blame you for being capitalist-minded. You couldn't help it, considering your background."

Another judge argued the case with me for half an hour one afternoon. He talked of a child from America and a child from Africa being placed in the same good school and home. When they grew up, they would be the same. I did not do much arguing, but I just did not believe that his case included all the facts. I did not believe it because my older brother and I had the same home and the same educational opportunities. He went to the Boston University School of Theology, while I went to Garrett Biblical Institute on Northwestern University's campus. That ought to have given me a considerable edge on him. But he has been the head of a theological seminary in South America for some twenty years, while the closest I ever got to such a position was as part-time teacher of New

Testament in a little theological college in West China. Of course, Boston gave him a trip to Europe and a Ph.D. They have a nice way about such little favors like that down Boston way. But I still think that his advantage was in the genes, not just the environment.

Probably I have a prejudice on this matter, though. Some thirty years ago I was pastor in a little town in Oklahoma. You knew there was a town because the sign-board on the highway said, "Lamont, Oklahoma, Population 402." There were two things you could say about that town. One was that every time a baby was born there the relative increase in population was much greater than when the same thing happened in New York City. The other was that the people there have hearts as big as their streets are wide—and dusty. Back in those days the Eugenics Society of America was strutting its stuff. My dictionary reads, "Eugenics is the improvement of the human species by properly planned miscegenation." The eugenicists figured that if Luther Burbank could improve roses and cacti, and chicken fanciers produce more eggs per hen, they ought to be able to improve the human race. So they were trying to inveigle all pastors into the support of their program by inviting us to write sermons on the subject and promising a prize for the best sermon. I bit, and wrote a sermon. But then I faced my hazard, for that sermon had to be preached. I knew I did not dare risk it on a morning congregation. I waited for a rainy evening when only the most loyal and intrepid spirits would venture out. The dryness of the subject would compensate for the wetness of the night. I preached my sermon. It made no great difference in the way the genes were distributed in that community, but it made a difference in my finances. For I won two hundred dollars as second prize, just at the time I had returned broke from a summer's vacation. I never told the people in Lamont about it for fear they would want to credit the money to the unpaid balance due the preacher. I just thanked the Lord, and sent twenty-five dollars to a Korean pastor whom I had known in Seminary. But ever since that time, while I am not as convinced that eugenics will save the world as my sermon indicated, I have had a friendly feeling for that cause and have been unwilling to go completely over to the side of the environmentalists.

But when the Communists talk of environment, they are not talking facts, but a faith. That is not to say that there are no facts on their side. There are plenty of them. You do not have to be a Communist to believe in the power of environment, social and economic influences, to mold character and civilization. The historian, Charles A. Beard, wrote a history of the United States based on this theory, and it is a good one. He was no Communist. The only trouble is that as a Communist you must believe that this is the only thing that counts. So if we all come out of the same pod, we are all as alike as peas. It is the equalitarian philosophy that has come to the top in every time of social upheaval, the French Revolution, the Russian, and now the Chinese. All facts are pressed into the Procrustean bed of this faith. Those facts that are too recalcitrant are ignored.

For Communism is fundamentally a faith. The Marxian philosophy with its jaw-breakers like "economic determinism," and "dialectical materialism," is a way of thinking that fits into this faith. Marx wrought it out of his own revolt against a European society that had spurned him. Lenin and others found in it a sharp sword to fight their battles. Their faith and hope and desire for social change needed a convincing apologetic. This they found in Marx and Engels. But if it were not for the faith that marches under the hammer and the sickle, the books of Marx and Engels would have been forgotten long ago.

To say that Communism is a faith will meet with some protest from its adherents, for it sounds as though I were going to call it a religion, and they are dead set against religion. Religion is nothing more than the vestigial remains of a decadent social order, and like the vermiform appendix, will someday be sloughed off and forgotten. But if religion be defined, not as the belief in God, but as that to which men give themselves in absolute devotion and loyalty, then Communism is a religion. We speak of those who make wealth their religion. During Hitler's regime, "blood and soil" were the dominant faith in Germany. Today in China Communism has erected new objects of loyalty and faith, and the fact that they are not molded as idols or require churches as centers of worship does not make them any less potent in their influence over the minds and hearts of millions. With the teachings of Marx and Engels as their holy book, Lenin as their prophet, and Mao Tze-tung and Stalin as their leaders, they are building the new day with the same starry-eyed enthusiasm and faith with which many Christians await the millennium. Almost every Communist activity can find its counterpart in the forms of worship and revival-ism of the West. Their huge parades dwarf the splendor and pomp of Catholic holy days, the massed banners of bright red more brilliant and impressive than cardinals' hats and robes, and the large pictures of the Communist hierarchy, blown up to several times life size, taking the place of "the host" in the processions. The emphasis on song as a way of teaching the ideas and implanting the loyalties of the new faith is the revival technique so well known and effectively used the world around. Their group life and study has its counterpart in youth camps and retreats. And over the radio on a patriotic day there come the voices and tears of those who have suffered under the heel of the old regime, recounting their losses and wrongs with a passion that rivals any testimony meeting that was ever held. Added to all this, Communism has the intoler-ance of a faith. Science is never intolerant, except intolerant of falsehood and intolerance. But faiths are often intolerant, especially when they are fighting for their foothold in the world.

It is because Communism is a crusading faith that it permits no criticism of its plans or programs. Under the Chiang regime, the English paper, *The Weekly China Review*, printed articles and editorials that scathingly denounced many of the things that the government was doing. The leading Chinese paper, *Ta Kung Pao*, did likewise, though it could not speak with the freedom of the English weekly. For some time there was even an avowed Communist paper published in Chungking. But this limited freedom, tolerated by the Chiang regime, would not be permitted for an instant under the present People's Government. All that is published is strictly censored, and no criticism of the policies and program of the government is permitted. Democracies gain strength from a rigorous opposition on the part of minorities. The critical voices of such liberal organs as *The New Republic* or *The Nation* are invaluable. But Communism does not believe in such freedom of the press any more than Fascism does. For it is a dictatorship that is determined to advance the ends of its new and intolerant faith. It permits no opposition.

Communism is not only a faith; it is a method of life. As I have seen it in China, it seems to me that this method might be summed up under learning, confession, group life, and hard work. It all starts with learning. From the very first every effort is made to convince the minds and change the way of thinking of the old order. Bookshops are crowded, and books are cheap. The books that are being sold are serious reading, and everyone is working furiously to learn the ways of the new day. In all of the larger stores, in banks, in public offices, and in schools, the daily hour of study is required. The newspapers carry serious articles on political, social, and economic subjects, usually one each day, and these articles often furnish the study material. These articles gear the Communist way of thinking into present-day problems, and help people to see why their poverty and hardships are due to the American imperialists of the West or to the landlords and profiteers that must be liquidated. All of the education is in the political, social, and economic fields, for that is where China's problems lie.

I have called this teaching "education," but "indoctrination" would be the truer word. I was to have nine and a half months of this "education" before I was released. I read a dozen books and spent hours each day in discussion with a group. But there could be no freedom of discussion, for any departure from the accepted dogma as set forth in newspapers or books was dangerous. Whether inside or outside the prison, one who has any independent ideas that vary in content or mode of expression from those set forth in the official literature is looked upon as a possible center of rebellion against the government, and is treated as a potential counterrevolutionary. Before any national anniversary, the government even prints a long list of slogans and cheers that can be used on that day. They are running no chances that the cheerleaders lead the crowds astray.

More than this, all information upon which discussion is based is carefully screened, and only that which the government accepts as "objectively true"—by which is meant that which advances the interests of the party—can be used as material for the learning classes. So the cowardice and ruthlessness of the American soldiers in Korea, the economic debacle in the United States where eighteen millions, or one half of the labor force, are now said to be out of work, the wonderful achievements of Russian science and industry as contrasted with the rapid deterioration of science in capitalistic countries, and the complete selfishness of everyone in capitalist societies, are a few of the "facts" which are reiterated day after day and which form the basis of all conclusions. If these "facts" are accepted as "true," and no one dares deny them, then the conclusions drawn from them are quite logical.

We once said that there could be no democracy in China until her millions could read and write. The Communists believe that an educated people are the bulwark, not of democracy, but of Communism. It is easier to direct an intelligent man, especially if you control all the avenues of information, than an ignorant one. So mass education is a must in the program. It is being promoted with great zeal. While in jail, I noted that the head of my soldier guards, who was himself a college graduate, spent every morning teaching the guards the equivalent of their A.B.C.'s. At the same time he drilled into them hate and fear of America.

All organs of education and propaganda are harnessed to this need for indoctrination. Radio, movie, handbills, song, the parade, and the drama all are made to serve this need. Even the paper sack that comes from the candy store carries a cartoon and the slogan, "Protect China! Oppose American imperialism!" One of the most powerful dramatic presentations I ever saw was *The White-haired Girl*, a story told in song and drama that is well known all over China today. It is the story of a peasant family suffering under the heel of a landlord, until the only daughter is seized in payment of debt and is compelled to work as a slave in the home of the landlord. There she is betrayed by the landlord's son. She flees to a cave, and lives in the darkness of that cave until the Liberation Army comes to free her and her community. Her hair turns white from the suffering. The dialogue is interspersed with songs sung in a minor key and accompanied by Chinese instruments. These songs have woven themselves into the thought and emotions of thousands, and their tunes and teaching can never be forgotten. The Communists know how to change mind-sets. Already most of the people have forgotten that the United States ever helped defeat Japan and think that it was all due to the People's Liberation Army and Russia.

Someone reported that when Dr. Hu Shih left Peking, before the Communists came in, and came to the United States, he remarked, "We didn't have freedom of speech under the Chiang regime, but at least we had freedom of thought." He was right there, for the Chiang regime, though a dictatorship under a thin veneer of democracy, never had the systematic thoroughness of the Communist organization. One corner of this control of thought rests on confession. The whole of society is broken down into these learning groups. But in addition to learning, there is discussion and confession. The great watchword is to be "*tang-peh*," or "frank." If you have had the wrong motive and done things that were evil before, that is nothing to be surprised at. That was because you were living in an evil society. But now you must change, and the first step is to confess your wrongs and start out with a clean sheet. Every day in the paper there are one or more confessions in which someone tells how he has wronged his employees, has taken money, or has done something else of which he is now ashamed. His confession is a sign that he has started anew.

All of those in the old regime who have come over into

the new and have been accepted could enter only by this door of sackcloth and ashes. One lady told me of a banker who was "invited" to one of the training camps where this retooling process was carried on. He was there several months, learning both by studying the new literature and by doing all his own coolie work just what the new order wanted. Day and night there was always a trusted "comrade" at his side, so that his every thought and attitude could be fully known and checked.

I have no way of knowing, but I doubt if there is much in the way of secret police. There would not need to be. For everyone knows everyone else's business in China. The people live too close together to have any of that highly prized privacy of the West. With everyone enrolled in learning groups, with confession a part of the program, and discussion always going on, anyone who refused to take part or who showed any contrary ideas would be spotted and reported. A person can express different opinions on minor matters, but not on any fundamental principles. There he must follow the Marxian line.

As I have indicated, everything is done through groups. At the prison I asked the guard to buy me a Bible. He took the request to the group and came back with a refusal. I would give money to one guard to buy candy and another would come with the candy. Thus they check on each other and know what each one is doing. They carry responsibility together. When the head of the guards came to see me about any important matter, he brought another man along with him. The leaders of the city government spend countless hours in committees, and my judgment is that everything is cleared through such committees. This probably goes clear up to the top. While Mao Tze-tung is the chairman, I feel sure that he makes very few independent decisions. Like all of the Communists, he probably expresses the decisions that are reached by the responsible committee at the head of government.

Add to these items the fact that everyone seems to have a job and be busy at it, and you have something of the picture of the methods that the Communists use. At the prison they also had the training center for several hundred new employees who were being processed before being sent to their tasks. Each day, over about a six-weeks' period, these young people from high schools and colleges were given full programs of song, study, speeches, and discussion from morning until bedtime, with a few breaks for play. The officials around the place would drag in at midnight or after, returning from full days in committees and work. There must be a tremendous lot of book work, records, and forms to do, as always wherever there is such control over society. No one was idle.

Whether the new government can furnish everyone with a job is a question that no one can answer yet. There is a limit to the number of employees even a Communist government can use, and unless there is an early and widespread revival of business and industry, there will be as serious unemployment among the graduates of high schools and colleges as there was under the Chiang regime. In the spring of 1952 the English magazine *People's China* announced that unemployment in China was no longer a problem. But in the summer, some three months later, the Chinese papers carried front-page news that the government was going to register all unemployed, and would do its best to meet a problem that had become serious. The truth seemed to be that no one knew the facts and that there was considerable unemployment which the government planned to remedy as soon as it was in a position to do so. Meanwhile, all employers were told they could not dismiss any employee without the consent of the factory committee and without first finding him a new job.

One thing the Communists have been trying to do is to break down the barrier between the scholar and the laborer. The laboring man is given a new status and called "comrade." If he can find some way to increase production in his factory or raise more rice per acre, he is voted a "hero of labor" and given a trip to Peking to see the big shots. I saw a truckload of these heroes in a parade one day. They did not look like heroes to me. But then, heroes seldom do. During the war we had some American soldiers in our home, and during the evening it developed that the least prepossessing fellow in the group had a letter of commendation from his general for pulling a flier out of a burning plane. He was there, saw the need, and met it. Probably he did not stop to calculate the risk he was running. So most heroes are a little slow in their mental processes and do not have sense enough to stay out of danger. When to everyone's surprise they come out in one piece, they are either heroes or martyrs—like me.

All students are required to do some rough labor. All of the personnel around the prison and those busy with the training groups, except for a few older men in more responsible positions, did their own washing with tub and washboard. My first guards who were college fellows boasted to me that they did manual labor. They seemed to think that I had never done any. They could not realize that in the United States for a man to pitch hay, repair his car, or mow his lawn is nothing to boast about, for it is our way of life. But for centuries trained mind and trained hand have never gone together in China. If the Communists get them together in the next few generations, they will have accomplished a major revolution.

While we are speaking of the barriers that the Communists are breaking down, perhaps we had better add another one or two. The inequalities of sex are being smashed. The Christian church has been working for years on this problem, educating the girls, and trying to implant new ideals in the Christian homes so the parents would be as happy over the arrival of a baby girl as they were over a boy. We had made real progress, but the task is gigantic and there is much to be done. Foot-binding is no longer practiced even in the rural areas, and in another generation it will be impossible to find any relic of this barbaric custom. The Communists have hitched their caterpillar trucks on to this problem of treatment of women, and have much more weight to pull society out of the mudhole of sex inequality than the church ever had. They have a new marriage code providing for monogamous marriage, based solely upon mutual affection and freedom of choice, a code which they are striving to enforce. All around the training center the girls were as plentiful as the boys, dressed in the same kind of cotton trousers and coat, and living in the same economical fashion. They were just "comrades," like the men, with no chance to put on make-up or anything else that would add to their sex appeal. In fact, everyone was so busy remaking the world that the matter of sex seemed to be shelved for the duration. I felt that no problems of irregularity could develop in that situation. Everyone was too busy, too happy, and too much involved in group life to permit such problems to develop, for on the whole, from the standpoint of sex, there was a much healthier atmosphere than on an American college campus. That does not mean that I am looking down my nose at the college campus, either.

Another barrier that is breaking, or at least beginning to crack under Communism, is family loyalty. This has always been the cornerstone of Chinese life. People could be excused for theft of public funds, for unlimited nepotism, and for almost any other crime if it were done for their families. During the war against Japan, the call went out for volunteers from the colleges. A large group volunteered from the colleges at Chengtu. But when they got through weeding out the physically unfit, they then weeded out the "only sons." For no boy would be asked to serve his country if he were the only son of his parents. That would be asking too much of family loyalty. The ones that remained were mighty few.

The Communists, with their customary realism, see this issue and are meeting it squarely. Those who enlist in the new government are shifted to places far from their own homes. Their income is so small that they cannot support their parents. They are drilled in the idea that country and cause are above home and family. Old customs of "favor" are out. One missionary came through Chungking with a note from some Chinese friend to a relative in the employ of the new government. The note did not help her, but very nearly queered her in her relation to authorities there. "Friendship pigeon" may not be entirely rooted out, but it is different from the "good old days."

One other item deserves a brief note. That concerns the working of women. The salaries paid by the government assume that husband and wife are both working. As the Board of Missions pays its missionaries double salary if married and single salary if single, so the People's Government. This creates a problem for the children, but that is met by having crèches, kindergartens, and primary and middle boarding schools. So parents, both of whom are working for the government or in industry, plan to part from their children when the child is about three, or even earlier, and the child is brought up with a greater sense of loyalty to the nation than to the home. This applies to only a small proportion of the total population, for most people are rural people who carry on their home life as before.

The fact that the women work is both an economic necessity and a way of breaking down old prejudices concerning "woman's place." In China, as in Russia, the government insists that for women to work is a virtue. But anywhere in the world where women are employed in large numbers in fields or factories, their employment is a sign of economic necessity. As soon as that necessity is over, or the urgency of war production is past, the women return to their homes. In China, the matter of women working has always been a spotted picture. On the Fukien coast, in the mountains where life is hard, the mountain women carry loads and work in the fields with their husbands. On the plain, where rice is plentiful and economic standards are higher, the women do not work in the fields, and have no notion that their mountain sisters have anything to boast about. At least, they did not yesterday. Perhaps Communism has changed that, too.

173

A faith and a method—that is Communism. If that were all, we could draw the picture in rosy outline and feel that China faced a very bright future. But Communism in China is also a movement that has a sense of mission, a responsibility toward the rest of the world. In this, Chinese Communism is one with Russian. And that's the rub.

The Mohammedan faith is propagated by the fanatical and proselyting zeal of its adherents. Communism spreads in the same way. All Communists are propagandists, preaching their doctrines to anyone who will listen. Their propaganda is a mixture of truths, half truths, and falsehoods woven together to convince the listener, and with little concern for scientific exactness.

There seems to be a peculiar twist in the human mind. When Communists are settling travel accounts or reporting income and outgo for government needs, they are meticulously exact. But when they defend their cause, they seek to convince you, not to state the truth.

One judge talked with me. I suggested that I preferred a democracy to a dictatorship and he immediately told me that I did not understand. China was fighting against feudalism, capitalistic profiteers, and American imperialism. But that left the main question of democracy unanswered. Another time when I suggested that the industrial order under capitalism seemed to be more efficient in economic production, he did the same trick. He first told me of some smart Russian scientist who had found a

way to stop all pain without the use of any drugs. I do not
know whether the method was hypnotism or an overdose
of vodka, but that makes little difference. Then he said
that in Russia, in thirty years, the country had jumped
from no industrial production to a place rivaling the United
States which had been at the job for a hundred and fifty
years. I did not bother to point out that to copy what someone else had done is much easier than to start from scratch,
that the October Revolution was made possible by factory
workers in Moscow who must have been employed in some
factories, and that Stalin himself had come up through the
ranks of industrial labor. If there had been no industry previous to Communism taking over, there would have been
no ranks for him to come up through. But these fairly
obvious facts are all ignored. Propaganda seems to anes-
thetize the critical faculties.

What is true of the individual Communist is even
more true when it comes to official propaganda. "Facts"
are manufactured with the greatest of ease, and the people have no way of checking them against any other facts.
Thus "the People's Liberation Army and Russia defeated
Japan," but for some unexplained reason let MacArthur
take over control. America, which had a piddling navy and
no major interest in China at that time, was "the cause of
the Opium War of 1840 and of foisting opium on China."
All history is rewritten to fit the present thesis of war
against American imperialism. "The United States is rid-

dled with Communism, with a strong minority of Congress being secret members of the Party. All the people of the United States are groaning under the burden imposed by Truman, Wall Street, and the sixty wealthy families." The picture that Malik draws of the situation in his tirades at the United Nations may seem off-center to you, but it is the only picture seen in Communist countries. All of it can be defended as a part of the "cold war" that may become "hot" any day.

When one has lived in the midst of this torrent of propaganda for a time he begins to doubt that anything from Communist countries is true. He greets it with the same skepticism my Chinese farmer friends greet my statement that in the United States we travel a mile a minute on streamlined trains and one farmer farms as much as a hundred acres all by himself. They have never been to America, but they know these things cannot be true. Likewise, I have never been to Russia. But I have lived in China, and I know that truth and propaganda are not on speaking terms there. I doubt if they are in Russia.

I have always puzzled over the diverse reports given by visitors to Russia or eastern Europe, but I understand that now. One goes with the measuring stick of industry in the States, and measures industry there by our standards of efficiency. His report is completely negative. Another goes with a sympathy for the Communist experiment and measures by their advance over a postwar chaos and economic collapse, and returns with a glowing report. The measuring sticks are different, and each sees what he is looking for. Both are true; yet neither is completely true.

If we were not living in a crowded world neighborhood, all of this falsification of the truth and building of unreal pictures of the world would make little difference. Two hundred years ago China's picture of the West was even more erroneous than it is today. But no one cared, for China was a long way off. That is not true today when the dogs of war are barking at our heels. That is why I left China with a heavy sense of pessimism, not as regards her internal affairs, but in relation to the international scene.

For an insane man is only one who is living in a dream world which has no touch with reality. He may be harmless. Or he may not be. Even so with a nation that builds, not on the stern realities, but on a world as she would like to have it. Remember Hitler and the ten years before the outbreak of World War II! In talking to one of my judges, I told him that I was pessimistic about the world situation, and that I, like all Americans, feared war. We knew what it would cost. His reply was, "We do not fear war. Wars are won by the infantry. Our People's Liberation Army can outfight the American troops. Your boys know more than Chiang's troops did, but they are poorly led and haven't any courage. The atomic bomb doesn't mean anything, for we have a diffused industry, not concentrated as in your big cities in America." He gave me a ten-minute oration

177

along this line. I sat there, dumb with amazement. When I think of the horrible shambles that would be left by a dozen well-placed atomic bombs in China, at Hankow, Shanghai, Canton, Tientsin, and strategic communication centers in Manchuria, and how quickly and effectively they would knock China out of any war, I cannot help but conclude that China has gone mad. That is the crux of the danger.

This is the danger, because for the first time in history a Chinese government has turned its foreign affairs over to another power. The voice that speaks from Peking on international issues is the voice of Moscow. Always before, people and students have protested any such subservience to another power. This time they are being sold the bill of goods that Russia is their great friend and benefactor and that they can escape from the big black wolf of Western imperialism only as they nestle in the protecting arms of the brown bear of the north. My guess is that the help secured from Russia in defeating Chiang's forces was conditioned upon this relationship being maintained. To mount such a tiger, as the Chinese say, is much easier than to get off.

Thus China has gained a friend to the north, but the price she has paid and will pay is very heavy. She has closed all doors to her recognition at the United Nations, has delayed for years any hope of getting Formosa back, has made the rearming of Japan inevitable, and has forfeited any chance of getting the large-scale economic help and trained Chinese personnel from the West necessary to develop her industries which alone can lift the economic burden from the shoulders of her struggling millions. Russia cannot supply this help, for the major part of her resources are absorbed in remaking her own national life. She has little to offer but advice.

So I left China with unalloyed admiration for the courage and reality with which the new government is facing the herculean task of remaking the ways of that great nation. No right-minded person can do other than wish for a better day for China's millions. But the questions that are raised by her sense of mission and consequent intolerance, and by her desire and determination to help in welding the whole world into one Communist state under Stalin, complicate the picture.

Back in 1936 I was riding with a missionary friend in that instrument of torture known as a West China bus, on a trip from Chengtu to Chungking. We were talking of Mussolini and his rule in Italy. My friend was enthusiastic about the new order in Italy and the progress that was being made. I agreed that some of his statements were true, but protested that a dictatorship and its sword-rattling spelled danger. The years have proved me right. Do we face the same thing in China today? A dictatorship that has no sense of mission may be burdensome to its people, but presents no threat to world peace. But when a dictatorship feels that all the world must be painted the same color, the hope of avoiding trouble is pretty slim. If Communism makes a few more moves like that in Korea, we may be plunged into a world war that will destroy all existing hopes and plans in China and in many other centers of the world as well. The one hope we have that this may not happen is the United Nations, backed by the preponderant power of the West.

9

Exit Missions

The arrest of a missionary in China on the charge of being a "spy" is a measure of the degree to which the climate has changed. The truth is that the ice age of Communism, as its critics would express it, has spread down from the north and covered China. In this age missions are finished.

The missionary enterprise of the Catholic Church in China is much older than that of the Protestant. Both groups expanded rapidly during the nineteenth and first half of the twentieth centuries. The rapidity of their growth was influenced by economic and political factors, but there was a steady, though uneven, increase in missionary personnel, investment, and membership up to the outbreak of World War II. In the early twenties the Protestants had more than six thousand missionaries in China, and the Catholics an even larger number. The Protestants boasted thirteen Christian colleges, scores of high schools and hospitals, and a membership of more than four hundred thousand persons. The Catholics were not so strong in the educational field, but had a larger church membership and were strongly entrenched in rural areas.

As one traveled across China there was almost no important city without its Gospel hall or its Catholic church. Occasionally the spire of the Catholic cathedral towered high above other buildings. The Protestant centers, while a bit shy on towers, were usually large and commodious as compared with the more crowded quarters of their neighbors. In county seat towns there were frequently the Western houses of missionaries, and close by, either a high school or a hospital, sometimes both. These have usually been impressively built in Western style. To be sure, compared to buildings in the States, they are quite modest, but then, few Chinese have ever been to the States. At each of these centers there was a goodly number of Christians, many of them employed in the multiplied activities of school, hospital, or evangelistic work. The relations between the foreign staff and the Chinese personnel were usually good, with no more difficulties than one would expect where people still retain their normal amount of human nature.

But now for several years the exodus of missionaries has been going on and is about finished. I was the last Methodist missionary to leave China. The China Inland Mission, which was the largest Protestant group of missionaries in China, had moved out more than nine hundred adults and children, leaving only eight not yet accounted for. They have changed their name to the Overseas Missionary Fellowship of the China Inland Mission, and are opening work in Japan, Formosa, and the South Seas. Other missions, both Protestant and Catholic, are doing much the same.

This exodus is different from any other such evacuation from China. China missionaries have always lived with one suitcase packed, metaphorically speaking. They never knew when they might have to leave. Nineteen hundred was the Boxer year; 1911, the overthrow of the Manchus and its attendant unrest; 1927, the advance of Chiang's armies and the trouble at Nanking; 1937, the outbreak of the Japanese war, with evacuation for some and internment for others. But this leave-taking is not the same. For this is no hurried exodus like the rest. Many missionaries left before the Communists arrived. Others have come out, a few at a time, but all are coming out and none going back. The government has protested that they were not against all missionaries, but just opposed to those who could not co-operate with the new regime. All who were "acceptable" might return. But when a Quaker, a single man who had proved his utter simplicity of life and co-operative spirit, reached Hong Kong, he could not get back to West China in spite of the fact that both students and local government at Chengtu approved his return. The reason given was that the Canton government did not know the man, and he would have to pass through Canton territory.

The opposition to the missionaries is not on the basis of anti-Christian or antireligious feeling. The People's Government guarantees religious freedom, and while Communism as a movement may be antireligious, denouncing all religion as harmful superstition, the government does not take that position officially. The bars are being put up against the missionaries purely and simply because they come from capitalist countries with which China is carrying on a "cold" war. Thus, if I had been shot as a "spy" at Chungking, I would not have died as a martyr to Christianity, but as a martyr to American capitalism. While I think that capitalism has a lot in its favor, the only time I ever voted was for Norman Thomas, and I object to dying for capitalism, American or any other type. But in China all missionaries, except a very few who have accepted or made peace with Communist propaganda, are now considered enemies of China's true interests.

The missionary institutions are reinterpreted in the same manner. In my trial hearings, more than one judge, when I protested that I had tried to be a true friend of China and had proved that friendship by raising thousands of dollars for schools and hospitals there, said that they considered such institutions the most subtle and dangerous organs of American imperialism. For they were deluding the people into believing that America was their friend, and setting up standards of life completely contrary to those promoted by Communism. They represented a cultural imperialism that was no less dangerous than economic and military imperialism.

In this matter the Communists are right, from their point

of view. If the world is to be divided into two camps with Communism on one side and capitalism on the other, then it is a war to the death and any failure to draw a sharp line and hold it is to give aid to the enemy. The very presence of missionaries and their money and institutions gives the lie to all propaganda that there is constant plotting for the destruction of the Chinese nation. Push the missionaries all out and in a few years it will be easy to make everyone believe that all people from capitalistic countries have horns and tails.

So the atmosphere has changed, almost all missionaries are gone, and institutions have passed into the hands of independent or government groups. All schools and hospitals are forbidden to have religious meetings of any kind or to give religious instruction. Students and nurses who want to have worship services or to organize religious fellowships among themselves can do so. But such actions will not make them very popular with their fellow students. That some continue to worship in groups is proof of the reality of their faith.

It is to be regretted that this exodus of missionaries from China has been accompanied by many unfortunate incidents which have deepened fear and hate and widened the chasm between China and the West. The government at Peking has evidently left all decisions regarding exit permits for foreigners in the hands of local officials. The result has been different decisions in different places. I was most

185

fortunate. Some missionaries have undergone torture. Some in need of medical attention have been denied exit permits until too late. All decisions, as far as the missionary could see, have been made in an arbitrary manner, the result depending upon the prejudices of the local officials. Unfortunately, the tide of war propaganda, fanning hatred of the West to white heat, was beating against all dikes of justice and fair-dealing, thus making any kind of generous attitude almost impossible. The treatment of missionaries, bad as it has been, has probably been better than we could have normally expected when all of the tragic factors in the situation are taken into consideration.

But missions are finished, and this will seem to most people a major tragedy. Certainly it is tragedy for most missionaries. Therefore, it may seem strange to have me say that I think the demise of the missionary movement in China may prove a blessing. It is quite possible that fifty years from now the church historian may write that this exodus of missionaries and the cutting off of the church and its institutions in China from their Western dependence was one of the major blessings of our age.

The umbilical cord that attaches Chinese Christianity to its Western mother had to be cut some time. The time would never have come when the separation would have been made voluntarily. In fact, the stronger the church in China became, the more it wanted from America and the more it got. Our Conference in West China was the youngest and perhaps the weakest in China Methodism. One would think that good sense and missionary strategy would have indicated the wisdom of letting the stronger conferences along the coast stand more on their own feet, while help was pumped into the weaker conference in the west. Not so! Missionaries to the west had to run the gauntlet of the coast where they might be tempted to remain. Money was divided, not on the basis of weakness and strength, but on the basis of the proportionate number of workers. So, in keeping with the words of the Master, "To everyone who has shall more be given," the stronger conferences got the larger amounts both in personnel and money.

This is not said in criticism, but to point out the fact that as long as it is possible to lean on someone else, no one no matter how strong is going to stand on his own feet. You could never have secured a majority vote of missionaries, to say nothing of their Chinese associates, that the time had come either to withdraw or to reduce aid to China. The only way Chinese Christianity will ever learn to stand on its own feet is by some such direct and brutal method as the present world tension provides. Like all other missionaries who have lived in China and learned to love that land and people, I regret that I cannot go back. But I believe that any change that would tempt the mission boards to go into China again within less than fifteen or twenty years would be a major catastrophe for the kingdom of God in that land.

187

After some twenty years, the church in China will be strong enough to stand a few missionaries and some financial help, with all controls fully in Chinese hands. But even then there may be danger of backsliding.

The church in China in this period must make great readjustments—to a totalitarian regime, to the absence of missionaries, to the lack of institutions, and to the end of subsidy from abroad. The adjustment to a totalitarian regime is difficult. This government today guarantees freedom of religious faith, but no one should assume that this "freedom" is the same as we enjoy in the United States or England. It is true that under this government there are no restrictions on the freedom of worship and assembly as long as the government is sure that pastor and people are loyal. But this is as far as the freedom goes. School books, newspapers, and other materials issued by the government are forthright in their opposition to religion as "the opiate of the people," and are scornful of all such useless superstitions as contrary to the truth and realism that is demanded in a scientific, progressive age. No government worker or comrade in either civil or military life goes to church without incurring the denunciation of his fellows. All students in high schools and colleges may secure financial help from the government to cover board, tuition, clothes, and incidental expenses, but upon graduation must plan to take such work as the government may dictate. Any young person who had received such help from the government would find difficulty in defending his desire to serve in the field of religion. Almost all books from capitalist countries are condemned as reactionary, so that the translation and circulation of such books is sharply curtailed. Thus the fountain of theological thought which has been watering the Christian plant in China is turned off. At the same time, the head of the Chinese government, Mao Tze-tung, is recognized not only as a political leader, but also as a philosophical thinker. His books, like those of Lenin and Stalin, often deal with a defense of dialectical materialism. The Christian church in China probably has only two or three leaders who are able to think and write in the field of philosophy and religion, and who would be able to cross swords with Mao Tze-tung and other protagonists of materialism. But they would not dare voice any such protest today. Add to all of these difficulties the fact that the church has been robbed of its hospitals, schools, and other institutions through which Christians could express their social passion, and one realizes that the "freedom of religious faith" in China is entirely different from what we know in the West. It is the kind of a freedom Communists say is enjoyed by laboring men in capitalist societies—the freedom to starve.

Like a little tree in a Japanese garden that has had its roots cut and has then been compressed into a pot, so is the church in China. It is still a church. It is still the Christian faith. But the steel bands of an unsympathetic, if not antagonistic, dictatorship prevent its full development into a creative, world-transforming, socially-redemptive force. Some time after "liberation," the Christian press at Shanghai sent out some material to be distributed to the churches. One item was the translation of a report on the Protestant church in Russia, probably written by that strong friend of the Communist cause, Dean Hewlett Johnson of Canterbury Cathedral. It told of the crowded churches and large gifts to the church by the Protestant worshipers in Russia. The figures looked screwy to me, but I am just naturally skeptical on all reports from Communist countries, whether they be "pro" or "anti." Buried in the report was a letter from the Russian church to their mother church, the Southern Baptists in the U.S.A., pleading with them not to spend so much time preaching the social gospel, but to stick to spiritual truth. I wonder what they would have said to us Methodists with our Federation for Social Action, and other agencies that are trying to interpret Jesus' exhortation to wash feet into terms of practical social service. At any rate, the advice is good—if you live under a totalitarian regime. For then you can do little or nothing about social problems, and had better concentrate on the job of changing hearts.

For the church in China to adjust to having no missionaries is more than a matter of not having foreign friends who will take a good deal of the responsibility and make many of the more unpleasant decisions. It is a cutting of the bond between East and West that has been so profit-able to both. This is a major loss for which nothing else can fully compensate. But the Chinese Christians are to a de-gree helpless in their situation. The government's propa-ganda organs have denounced all missionaries, and the only way in which the Chinese leadership could both keep out of jail and retain influence in the Christian movement was to echo this voice of vituperation. So I, as other mis-sionaries, have seen friend after friend lend their voices to denunciation. I could understand, for they had to choose between defending their foreign friends and being free to continue in the Christian movement. I can only guess the social pressures which have been brought to bear upon them and what their action has cost them.

The loss by the church of its institutions was inevitable. These institutions, hospitals and schools, are completely under the control of the government, and now that all financial aid from abroad has been stopped, have become government institutions. The schools continue to teach, and the hospitals to heal, but they no longer do it in the name of Christ. During the summer of 1952, the government announced that all colleges would be reorganized and fitted into an all-China plan which would make for econ-omy and efficiency. The church colleges, which comprise about one tenth of the higher educational institutions in China, have changed their names so that people can soon forget that they were ever related to the Christian movement. Each institution is to specialize, West China Union University concentrating on medicine and dentistry only, Szechwan University providing for arts and sciences, Chungking University offering engineering, and other schools specializing in business administration, agriculture, music, or other fields of education. Thus money and personnel can be used with the greatest efficiency. Since the government is meeting all expenses, salaries of teachers, administration, and subsidies for the students, it transfers teachers from school to school as it may see fit. This is a good policy and is fairly easy to do when all power is in the hands of the government.

But this loss of institutions does not mean that all of our investment in hospitals and schools over the decades is wasted. The hospitals are open and the schools still crowded, though they are not making the Christian witness we desire. But more than this, we must not overlook the great contribution that they have made in the creation of Christian leadership over the years. Lydia Trimble is known as the woman who put her life into the building of Hwa Nan College for Women at Foochow. During the war against Japan she was living in Foochow, having retired but not willing to leave the land of her adoption. One night one of the main college buildings caught fire. As she stood with the crowd watching it burn, one of her students cried, "Oh, Doctor Trimble, Hwa Nan is burning." "Hwa Nan burning?" retorted Miss Trimble. "Hwa Nan cannot burn.

Hwa Nan is the hundreds of women who have graduated from her halls and are serving all over China. Hwa Nan is a spirit, a life incarnate in her alumnae. That cannot burn." It is well to remember that this pronouncement can be made of other colleges as well.

This loss of institutions, moreover, is not entirely on the debit side of the ledger. Ever since the famous Laymen's Enquiry and Report some twenty years ago, the Boards have known that the church in China had a much larger institutional growth than it had Christian rootage. The situation was better in other parts of China than in the West China Conference, but everywhere this charge was in some degree true. In West China we have a Conference of only some twenty-five to thirty active pastors serving in about forty churches. Yet we boasted eight high schools, four hospitals, six or eight rural health centers, a midwifery training center, and a fifth share in a theological college and a university. One third of the members of the Conference were on the retired list, one third in institutional work of one kind or another, and one third actually engaged in evangelistic work. In the work of the women, almost all of their attention was given to medical and educational activity. The bishop spent the major part of his time on institutional problems, and Conference sessions did likewise. All of this institutional growth was good, and it was serving the Chinese people. But it was not the fruit of the Chinese church, but of the American church. The growth in this field was so luxuriant that it tended to overshadow the primary need of building the church. Now with the institutions cut off from the church, perhaps the eyes of the Christian group may be concentrated on their primary task of proclaiming the Word.

Little more needs to be said about the adjustments that must be made to lack of financial help from abroad. When this financial help was cut off, the church in China launched a movement for self-support, self-government, and self-propagation. How well they have succeeded in securing larger gifts from the church membership, I do not know. The church will have to restudy its methods, probably depending more on a volunteer lay pastorate. It will have to preach the gospel of stewardship with more zeal. But it can do that. Vitality is not a matter of financial resources, but of consecration and religious depth. Some of the more conservative groups in China have been self-supporting for years. One has a medicine factory at Shanghai and its apostles sell medicines as they move from place to place proclaiming the Gospel.

The future for the church in China depends on the Christians there having a vital Christian faith. For Communism is dogmatic and intolerant. It knows what it believes and preaches it with conviction. Any Christian who is on the fence or is wobbling in his belief will be pushed off and will probably fall into the snare of the Communists. Some of my Chinese friends who were quite emphatic in their denial of the messianic claims of Jesus are now enrolled in the ranks of a messianic Communism. In this situation the Christian liberal has no chance of survival unless he has a faith that is fed by the fires of a flaming mysticism. The dogmatic Fundamentalist and conservative has an easier time of it. He knows where he stands. He believes that Christ will return and that his one job is to proclaim Christ until he comes again. He has a dogmatism to set against the dogmatic claims of Communism. He will not win any convinced Communist, but neither will he surrender the fort. He will live, and his number will grow. He will not let the light of the Gospel die in China. Though we may not agree with him, his value to the Christian cause is beyond compute. For the kernel of Christian truth is his. May his tribe increase! After which I cannot help but add a sage remark made by an old friend, Roderick Scott of Fukien Christian University, some twenty years ago. He said, "You know, there is really not so much difference between the apocalypticism of a Seventh Day Adventist and a Communist. They have many things in common."

The church in China today faces its new challenges with a good deal in the way of resources. There is the open Bible, well translated and well known. The Christian press is still there, and will continue to produce some Christian literature. The union hymnal that was finished about fifteen years ago is invaluable. The theological training is being concentrated at Nanking and is being prostituted to gov-

ernment ends. But patience and courage on the part of the
Chinese Christians may yet unsnarl this difficulty. There is
a fairly large group of able leaders in the Christian movement, and we may have confidence that though they may
bend to the adverse winds that blow today, they will not
surrender their Christian faith or witness. More than this,
there is a great body of Christian people, many of them
tracing their Christian heritage back through three or four
generations. It is true that a large number of youth in the
churches are following the Pied Piper of the New Order.
There has been a shrinkage in membership. But this has
happened in other crises in China, and each time of difficulty has resulted in a deepening of the spiritual life. For
some reason, the Christian plant seems to grow best in the
arid sands of adversity. We need not fear. The church today has more in the way of resources than at any other
time of missionary evacuation. It will stand.

There are two other facts that make me confident of the
future of the Chinese church. One is the fact that Christianity is offering something that Communism does not
have. It speaks to an area of life that Communism has left
untouched. Social, political, and economic reform are all
necessary. But they are not the whole of life. After a few
nore years of concentration on those questions, people will
be wanting a change in diet. The fundamental hunger will
persist. From whence do we come? Why are we here?
Whither are we going? What is the basic answer to life's

agony and pain and hunger and striving? These questions Communism ignores. It says they do not matter. But life has a way of forcing us to face them. Christianity alone has the answer, an answer that makes sense. That is one of the reasons that when the Communists say "antireligious," they mean "anti-Christian." For they know that Christianity is the only faith in the world that presents any live alternative to their materialistic determinism.

The other fact is the grace of God. Turn back to the time of the French Revolution and the Deists and you can find a replica of the China picture today. Then they killed the church and buried her. But she did not stay dead. They treated her the way West China farmers treat their sugar-cane tops. They cut them off at harvest time and bury them in a long trench. They are dead. But in the spring they dig them up and lay them out in shallow rows and cover them with a little dirt. In a few days sun and rain awaken them. They send forth shoots and send down roots. They are alive. Even so the sunshine and rain of God's grace and mercy are in China, pouring life into many a Christian heart. Sherwood Eddy wrote a book entitled *I Saw God at Work in China*. I not only saw God there, but felt the power of His grace. From my own experience I know what God can do for one who is in real need. Therefore, I know what He can and will do for the church in that great and needy land.

10

Time Shuffles Along

My ninth month closed with no release. I was disappointed, but could do nothing about it other than to continue to trust God. The next day was Monday, and Dr. Stewart Allen and I paced the exercise court for fifteen minutes in the morning, smiling at each other but not daring to speak. Tuesday morning I paced it alone. Stewart was gone, and I assumed that he was released after eight months and five days. I learned later that he was transferred to another prison, and actually was not permitted to leave China until four months later. But he was no longer my neighbor. This meant that I was the only American left. The Chungking zoo which had housed three foreign "high noses," the largest number ever in captivity in that city, had shrunk to one lone survivor. Surely he was not worth keeping. After all, it had been a pretty poor show.

A week later as I was getting ready for bed, a guard came in with the request that I write down the date I had come to prison and how long I had been there. I wrote that I had been in jail nine months and nine days, having been arrested on the 26th of the previous November.

I did not sleep too well that night, for I was sure something important was being decided. On the morning of the second day my suspicions were confirmed when one of the guards brought me, not rice gruel or milk, but a high-class breakfast of rice, vegetables, and soup. He gave it to me with a smirk on his face as if to say, "This is your farewell meal." I was so sure of it that I deflated my air mattress and packed some of my gear. But the doors did not open. I waited all day, too anxious to do any serious reading or writing. Nothing happened. Someone had thrown a monkey wrench into the machinery.

Two weeks later I was aroused at night for another question period. The judge had quite a list of questions, most of which had been cleared before. He was so anxious to finish things that, having failed to get them done in two hours that night, he set the next day for a continuation of the inquiry. That was the first time in nine months when any judge seemed determined to finish the trials. We met the next day, and completed the list. I hoped this was the end and my release would not be postponed much longer.

One minor difficulty of those closing inquiries related to Pastor Chu, pronounced "ju" as in "Judas." He was a maverick that had strayed over into the Methodist herd, and was welcomed because he was far above the average of our pastors in education and preaching ability. His one

big fault was that he was bone lazy. He had been offended
when the new regime came along and made impossible the
continuation of the student church which he had served.
The bishop appointed him to another charge, but he refused to go and became quite incensed because we wanted
to apply the rule, "no work, no salary." Meanwhile, he had
got crosswise with a number of Chinese ladies on the high
school campus. So he issued a dodger that covered the
whole situation, accusing me of being a "foreign spy" and
the four ladies of being "running dogs of the foreigner."
The ladies took the matter to court and made him apolo-
gize in the paper. But I had no standing at the court and
could do nothing but keep my patience and wait. A few
weeks later he left town and I thought my relations with
him were over. But I did not know my man.

Late in the fifth or sixth month of my imprisonment the
official inquisitor came in one day, showed me a copy of a
sheet of squares, letters, and figures which he said was a
secret code which I had mailed in one of my letters to
Hong Kong. I told him he was a liar, in as polite Chinese
as I could, and stood by my guns. I had never seen the
paper before. That "code" kept coming up in every hearing from then on. But it was not until late in the game that
they gave me enough information about how and when it
was mailed to enable me to crack the mystery.

I then told them what I was certain had happened.
Pastor Chu had accused me of being a spy. So he manu-

factured his proof. He went into my office, borrowed my typewriter to copy several harmless articles on China, to which he forged my name. He then created this "code" which would further confuse the police. He stole several envelopes from my desk that had my name and return address on them, and mailed them all in the post office where he knew all my outgoing mail would be censored. All neat and sure fire! I pointed out to the judge that I never signed an article in that way, but always sent an accompanying letter. I showed him that the arabic figures on the "code" were written by a Chinese, drawn with the same care that a Chinese writes his characters, and lacking those flourishes that lend polish and uncertainty to figures I write. And I proved to them that Chu was the only man around who had the knowledge of English, access to my office, and sufficient motive to do such a dirty trick. My explanation, I thought, was accepted. I hope that the magic environmental influence of the New Order will change Pastor Judas into an honest man. Otherwise he is sure going to have trouble squeezing by St. Peter at the pearly gates.

I continued to wait. Nearly four weeks later this judge who had held the last inquiry popped into my room. He said that the authorities had received seven million dollars —about two hundred U.S.—from my wife for me, and that I could get the money when released. That word told me what I had guessed from some other things which had happened and from my knowledge of Esther's good sense, namely, that she had left China. Fortunately for my peace of mind, I did not know that she had suffered five months of persecution at the hands of patriotic students and soldiers who made spasmodic searches of the house, frightened the servants into quitting, and then made it almost impossible for her to buy food. I did not know that she had had to pack up and move out on two days' notice, finding refuge at the Rackhams' in the city, and that she had lived there through a long period of tension and uncertainty, knowing nothing of my condition nor when she might be permitted to leave China. I did not know that from the upstairs porch of the Rackham house she could look across the river and see public executions of Chinese prisoners again and again, with no certainty that I would not be included in the next lot. If I had known all of this, and that after she left China she had gone on to Hong Kong to wait for nearly a year, meeting the train from Canton day after day in the hope that I might be on it—if I had known what my imprisonment was costing her, I would have found it much more difficult. For her, as for me, only the sustaining grace of God had made sanity and courage possible.

This judge who had come in sat down and discussed my case with me. He said that none of the judges had found anything to object to in any of my answers or in the materials that I had written. All of the rest had voted that I might be released. But he felt that it was uncertain that my conduct after I left China would be helpful to the Communist cause. So the other judges had agreed that my further detention would be left wholly to his judgment. I didn't ask him how further detention on the basis of his hunch would make me more friendly to Communism. I had to assume that he owned some kind of crystal ball in which he could read future events. As Christians we assume that the future is known to God alone. But if you do not believe in God, the only thing to do is to arrogate to yourself such omniscience.

On leaving, this judge asked me to write another "confession." This I did. He came in the next day, saying my first attempt at confessing had not been detailed enough, and that I was to try again. He also left me two English magazines so that I could clear up my thinking on Communism. In reading these I learned for the first time that the war in Korea was still going on, but that peace was being talked. I wrote another confession and sent it in, but had no hope it would pry open the prison door. For I had learned some months before being arrested that one of the judges was a personal friend of the head of the Commercial College who had accused me in the first place. This was evidently the man, and my release would not depend upon anything I wrote or said, but upon the prejudice and hate of that school group. Certainly I would be in for a full year, and perhaps longer. Which led me to observe that though the good ship "Justice" may be driven from its course by winds of prejudice and hate or by the strong tides of special privilege, power, and wealth, it has some hope of making harbor as long as it has the chart of constitutional law and the rudder of trial by jury and right of appeal. But when these have been jettisoned, there is little probability that "Justice" can escape disaster, no matter how good the compass of conscience may be.

So I continued to wait. I thought of the phrase "Time marches on"; but for me, it shuffled along, minute by minute and hour by hour, oftentimes seeming to stand still. I think the guards felt special sympathy for me, for one of them came offering to open again the privilege of buying candy and fruit for me. I appreciated that, and sent for peanut candy, and later for tangerines. The food improved with cooler weather, the days were shorter, and life, though still difficult, became easier than during the first months of imprisonment. It turned cold, even snowing a skift on Thanksgiving Day. I went back into my airman's lined trousers and my one pair of winter pajamas for both sleeping and winter underwear. Only my air mattress seemed to be weary of the long wait and every night would literally let me down. The days continued to drag and the end of the first twelve months was near.

As I looked back over the year, I could feel nothing but a deep sense of gratitude to God for the way in which He had sustained me day after day. There were hawkers on the street selling hot water each morning. Their calls greeted me, sounding exactly like "How do you like it? How do you like it?" Such insulting remarks could only be answered by asserting that I did not like it and wished I were out. There were times of emotional depression. But they were few, and the way in which God's grace continued was a miracle such as I had never dreamed possible. His grace sharpens all faculties, including the sense of humor. If a deeper religious experience robs one of his ability to see a joke, even when the joke may be labeled "for private reading only," that experience is shoddy.

My imprisonment was, by any standards of justice that we know in the West, completely unjust. The solitary and indeterminate features of it were unnecessary and cruel. The arbitrary decision of one judge to hold me in prison for months after the other judges had voted my release was an expression of petty tyranny that cannot be defended on any basis. Yet every one of those difficulties was used of God for creative ends. If I had had a companion in my cell, or all the books I wanted to read, I would have written nothing and would have seen little that was new in the New Testament. If I had had anything else to do, I would not have tried my hand at poetry in the summer and would have missed one of the most exciting experiences of my life. And if I had been released at the end of the nine months as the majority of the judges voted, I would never have written this story.

Somehow every difficulty and disappointment became a road to greater achievement.

Very few of my prayers were answered during those months in the way that I prayed them. I had prayed that Dr. Stewart Allen might get out before I did, even though he had arrived at the prison nearly a month later, for I felt he had had a much tougher time of it, having no New Testament and no opportunities to write, and having no air mattress. His days must have been horribly long. God answered that prayer. I prayed that my prison experience might be used creatively for Kingdom building, and God is still busy answering that prayer. But every time I prayed that the doors might open, He answered my prayer, not by giving me what I asked, but by giving me another gift of His love and grace. It was like a child who asks his mother for the meat cleaver, and she very wisely gives him a bright trinket instead—much more fun and quite harmless.

I prayed for a Methodist hymnal. None came in, but God quickened my memory to write down a list of more than one hundred and twenty hymns and choruses I could use instead. I prayed for a whole Bible. None came, but God led me to search the New Testament more diligently and write nearly a hundred devotional talks. Again and again I hoped for a day of release and prayed that it might happen, only to have the petition denied. One or two months later I would look back upon what had been accomplished and thank God for His goodness in keeping me in jail. That was true all the way through. Summer with its nightmare of heat and bedbugs became a chance to show me what He could do. It was like a scientist who isolates his experiment in a laboratory so that all other factors can be cut out and he will know what causes produce what results. So I was isolated from friends, books, music, beauty, and all else. Then God proved to me that what I got did not come from anywhere else than from His mercy and grace.

I cannot explain all of this any more than I can explain electricity. All I know is that it happened. During the last three months of that first year I reviewed all of my poetry and my devotional talks. The latter I had so well in mind that I knew I could rewrite them when I was released, and I memorized the index for my poetry so that I could continue to review it without any written aid of any kind. I was coasting along toward the end of the year with no thought of doing any more writing. Then God spoke again.

Pacing my cell one day and thinking about what had been done, I received a flash to take the articles I had written on the Gospel of John and expand them into a small book on "The Gospel of John by a Prison Window." At first I protested that the material was not enough. But I set to work and found more. I did not know whether my idea on John as a different type of literature was too shopworn to use or not. I knew I had had courses on John, but no one had ever spoken of John as a completely different type of literature. Anyhow, I would put the material into shape and see if any publisher could be inveigled into printing it. I had hardly finished with John until the second flash came. This one was almost like an electric shock. The orders this time were to write up my prison experience. Again I protested that I did not have enough to say and that no one would read it. But I sat down, and in half an hour had the chapter headings for this book. I saw how it could be done. But was it wise? I did not want to send to the street for more notebooks and ink. My ink bottle was nearly empty, not more than half a dozen fillings. I decided that I could use the broad margins of my anthology of poetry and would write until my ink gave out. Some things would have to wait until I got home, anyhow.

I started in. I have never had so much fun writing anything. I would go to bed at eight in the evening, only to waken at two in the morning with my mind crowded with memories and stories that could make the day's writing. I would lie there on my cot, waiting impatiently for daylight to come so that I could get release from the burden that was on my mind. As soon as I got it down, I was free to think of something else. Thus in two-weeks' time the major part of this book was written on the margins of the anthology of poetry.

Please do not misunderstand me. I do not have any private wire to heaven. When my friend Will Schubert used to talk of God's guidance, I listened with the same kind of skepticism with which you may have been reading these words. I was always willing to seek God's advice and then follow my own judgment. And to talk of God's guidance always seemed to me to run into the danger of boasting that you had special access to Headquarters, or to lead you to make independent decisions with little regard for other people's opinions. So I listened to those who talked of God's guidance with a good deal of reservation.

But not now. I have had too deep an experience and have seen a miracle happen that I cannot shrug off. I have learned as I never knew before the tissue-paper thinness of the veil between us and the spiritual world. This does not mean that I shall ignore the advice of friends or fail to seek their help in important matters. I believe God leads them as truly as He leads me, and often when they are not aware of it. I pray that my own deeper sense of God's guidance does not make me less co-operative and humble. If it does, it is not worth a plugged nickel. But I cannot deny the spiritual birthright which God had vouchsafed to me over those months, nor believe that the same experience is not possible to every humble believer who admits his need and in humility and love seeks the "inner light." Even as I pen these lines by a prison window, I pray that more than one reader will do as I have done and find that the well of living water is one that never runs dry.

The end of the first twelve months came with no release.

209

But I hardly expected that the doors would open exactly on schedule. For that would have seemed as if I had had a fixed sentence of one year, and would have been too much like the decadent custom of fixed sentences customary in capitalist countries. I thought that it would probably happen a week or so later. Then looking at my calendar, I realized that the judge had told me they had received the seven millions from my wife on October 10. They had put the money into the bank, probably getting 2½ per cent per month interest, thus collecting enough to cover my board bill. They would not take it out before the end of the month and thus lose their interest. I thought that if Esther had been so unwise as to send me twice as much money I would have been such a profitable asset that I never would have been released. So I settled down to wait for the police bureau to collect their interest.

Haircut and shave were postponed. I had ben getting them every six weeks during the fall, but more than seven weeks slipped by before the 10th of December rolled around. It would not pay to give me a haircut and a shave and then have to repeat them a week later, for they cost the whole of five cents. On the final day, the barber arrived—and also another of those special breakfasts that would be a farewell meal. Again I deflated my air mattress and packed my gear. And again I waited through a long day of disappointment. The doors did not open.

The bitter hopelessness of that experience drove me to

face the reality of the situation with a new earnestness. It seemed perfectly clear to me that I had no hope of being released for months so long as the teachers and students of the Commercial College retained their hate and vindictive spirit. The judge who had full power in the matter would do what they wanted. No one on the outside knew the full facts or could do anything if he did know. There seemed only one thing to do, and I had no guarantee that it would bring results. But it was Christian, and was wise. I was convinced that the only thing that could break the log jam of malice and ill-will was the dynamite of aggressive love, the doctrine of the second mile expressed in a concrete and completely sincere way.

So I secured ink and paper from the guard and wrote a long request to the prison authorities. I asked them to translate and give to the Commercial College my deep regret over the whole situation that had caused them to hate me. I pointed out that I had not been primarily responsible for the decisions that had brought hardship and injustice upon them, and that I had no power to change those decisions. But I did regret them and did feel that some of them had been unfair. I was sorry for the actions taken and for any share I had had in them. I did not want another Christmas season to pass without having done everything I could to clear up misunderstanding and hate, and to prove to them that I counted them as my friends, and wished them every success in their school. To prove the sincerity of my own attitude, I would make a personal gift to the Commercial College of five hundred dollars U.S. as promptly as I could after being released from jail and before I left Chungking to return to America. For I was unhappy to close my missionary career in China with the knowledge that any group of Chinese teachers and students felt I had been other than both just and friendly in my dealing with them. Having written this statement with as much care as I could I turned it in with the prayer that God would help those who read it to believe in my sincerity and true friendliness.

A week later, just twelve months and twenty-three days after my arrest, a lady secretary came to my room with the final bill of particulars, giving the findings of the court. These stated that I had received gifts from the American consulate when they left, and from the J.C.R.R., that I had listened to the Voice of America and had sent news of the world situation to missionary colleagues in country stations, and that I had written things in my letters that showed that I did not have a proper respect for the People's Government and that reflected a capitalistic mind. All of these were true, and I signed the paper to indicate I agreed with these findings. There was not one word stating that I was a spy, had had special relations with Mr. Moosa, the A.P. correspondent, or with Senator Knowland, or that I had received any money from Chiang Kai-shek. But this list of findings that was finally squeezed out of the dozen or more inquiries kept me in solitary imprisonment for more than a year.

My second Christmas came and went with as little attention as a speeding motorist gives to a Burma Shave sign along the highway. Since it was a religious festival, none of the Communist staff or guards knew it had come. The Christian Chinese prisoner in the next room, a man whom I had never seen before, tuned up his rich baritone and gave me a private concert on Christmas Eve, going through the familiar Christmas carols and arias from *The Messiah,* ending with a good strong singing of "Merry Christmas to you." The next morning I responded in kind, though with much less tonal quality. A single prison-made Christmas card was surreptitiously thrust into my transom, greetings from another Christian prisoner. I did not dare reciprocate. Special eats for the day consisted of ten cents' worth of large tangerines, sixteen in all.

Time continued to shuffle along. Chinese New Year, which is determined by the moon calendar and usually occurs about a month after our Western New Year, crept nearer. From my peephole at the window, I could see the people on the street washing their clothes, cleaning their houses, and preparing rice cakes for the New Year festival. On Saturday morning, January 26, just exactly fourteen months from the day I had been arrested, the guards came in to tell me to pack up my stuff. I was moving. I did not know whether this meant release, or further imprisonment. I had been disappointed so often that I did not dare hope for complete release. But I packed up my things, whistled the tune of "God Be with You until We Meet Again," so that the prisoner next door could know I was leaving, and shouldering sleeping bag and clothes, went forth to face the unknown.

11

John the Baptist, Streamlined

One hour later, after a fifteen-mile ride in a jeep, with handcuffs on wrists and a fully armed guard on each side, I landed in the Southwest prison for counterrevolutionaries on the outskirts of Chungking. I was to learn later that this is a large prison farm, including coal mine, truck gardens and rice fields, and with all kinds of small productive enterprises, all manned by prison labor and virtually self-supporting. After being separated from all my books, including the New Testament, my watch and wedding ring, my pens and pencil, and everything else save toothbrush, clothes, and bedding, I was conducted to a ten-by-ten room, introduced to seven other prisoners, and assigned to one corner as my living space. With eight of us in the room, no one dared take any more space than was necessary.

Life there was a down-to-the-earth existence. We lived on the floor, ate on the floor, slept on the floor, and exercised on the floor, Japanese style. Shoes were parked in the hallway and rice bowls and wash basins parked outside at night. That floor was washed several times a day and we vied with one another to keep it dustless. In the daytime we would roll up our bedding and sit on it; at night we rolled it out for sleeping. My air mattress and six feet of bodily extension created a problem, but the man opposite me was short and willing to adjust. So we slept, packed together as tight as bugs in a rug, and no one complained. We did not dare.

I had often heard girl friends talk about the joys of a slumber party, and had thought maybe I had missed something. But somehow this slumber party lacked the hilarity that I had always associated with such an experience. Perhaps it was because the participants did not appreciate the fun of sleeping on the floor. Or perhaps the deterrent was the twenty commandments posted on the wall.

Those commandments were certainly a wet blanket on the spirits of the prisoners. They were detailed and specific, covering all phases of prison life. Each prisoner had to memorize them and each evening we reviewed them. They forbade us to move from our places in the room, ordered us to be polite to all the "government gentlemen" and guards, to protect public property and health, to report anything that we saw or heard of counterrevolutionary activities on the part of fellow prisoners, and to spend our time thinking about our sins and confessing them to the proper authorities. We were forbidden to laugh, whistle, or sing, or do anything that would show we were not living in a spirit of repentance. Most important of all we were to reconstruct our own thinking and attitudes until we stood with "the enlightened people" of the world. Those commandments were certainly a headache. To make matters worse, a guard marched up to the door about every ten minutes, day and night, and listened to all that was being done or said. Any collusion among the prisoners or any speech or action of a subversive nature would be spotted immediately.

The controls continued through the night. If you were uncomfortable at night, you waited until you heard the guard approaching along the corridor. Then you shouted out, "Report: Little convenience!" Which, being interpreted, meant, "I want to announce that I'm suffering considerable inconvenience." It reminded me of the third grade in school when we would raise an embarrassed hand and pipe up, "Please, teacher, may I be excused?" If you heard a grunt from the guard you knew that your "report" had been acknowledged and you could arise. But if you arose without that grunt of permission you got into trouble. I made a slip one night, and had to stand for ten minutes before the door while the guard lectured at me through the peephole. I still think that he just wanted an opportunity to see what a bearded foreigner looked like dressed in mottled green nylon pajamas. He probably had never seen such nightwear—or any kind of nightwear—before.

The only emergency not covered by the written rules was spitting. The Chinese are the world's champion spitters, and to have demanded that they "report" every time they wanted to use the cuspidor would have required a tripling of the guards to cover the emergency. Smoking, wine, and gambling were all forbidden, an easy rule to enforce since all money had been impounded by the authorities and no tobacco or wine could be purchased.

The food, served twice a day, consisted of rice and one vegetable, with a small bit of meat twice a month. Since all came from the prison farm, one vegetable would be served meal after meal until the season for that vegetable had passed. Thus spinach, cooked in a little salt water with a little lard added occasionally, continued for twice a day over about three months. I could stow away a pint and a half of rice and half a pint of vegetable twice a day with no particular difficulty. The prisoners all said that this was the diet of the average Chinese farmer and that we were fortunate to be treated so well. It was a considerable drop from the diet standard I had had over the first fourteen months of solitary. So we ate, squatting on our haunches around the central vegetable bowl, rice bowls and chopsticks in hand, chomping, slurping, gulping, and burping our way through the meal. Orders forbade all conversation, but this did not mean that the meal was eaten in silence.

But the important thing was to clear my case. One of

the G.G.'s (short for Government Gentlemen) called me into another room, told me that this was the highest prison authority in Southwest China, that I had failed to tell the truth during my fourteen months in the Chungking city jail, and that now I must settle down to the task of reconstructing my thinking and admitting my crimes. My fellow prisoners, who called themselves my "fellow students," assured me that they would help all they could, that they had a responsibility to the Chinese people to see that I changed from an enemy into a friend so that if and when I left China I would stand with the great dispossessed masses of the world in their struggle to throw off the shackles of capitalistic exploitation. The important thing for me to do was to see what kind of a world I was living in and to change my attitude from counterrevolutionary to prorevolutionary. It looked to me like a big job, to convert a dyed-in-the-wool patriot and capitalist like me. But I assured them that I would do my best to see my faults and correct them.

The "students" and the G.G.'s all recognized my difficulties, but this did not discourage them. Each day we spent the hours reading Communist literature aloud and discussing the truth we found there. At first I raised objections to certain statements. That was just what the rest hoped I would do. This provided a wonderful opportunity to harangue me upon my false views, to blaze out in hate against America and capitalism, and to show me where I was completely wrong. The room crackled with hate, a new China that I had never seen before. I was their enemy. I can close my eyes and hear them again as one after another recited my sins and told me what America had done to China.

"You are an imperialist," one man shouted. "You came to China to preach religion. But that was only to deceive the people. The great mass of the people were under the heel of a feudalistic landlordism, a life that was little better than slavery. This system was supported by the United States and other foreign powers. When we arose to throw off these chains of exploitation and oppression, the United States loaned money, planes, military equipment, and personnel to the Bandit Chiang Kai-shek to stop us. You approved of that. You preached religion, but you were using it as a blind, deceiving the students and farmers of China into thinking the United States was their friend. You were worse than those who took guns out and killed Communists, for you were leading thousands astray with your Christian propaganda."

"Yes," continued another prisoner, "and what has your Christian civilization brought China? Opium, syphilis, and bedbugs—those are the three contributions of your vaunted Western civilization. If you had got off our necks, we could have had this revolution thirty years or more ago, could have built a new China then, and would have avoided making the mistakes that have landed us in jail.

Not only the sufferings of China as a whole, but also our own personal problems were all created by your imperialistic America."

"And see what the United States is doing today," said another. He stuttered when he talked, taking about twice as long to make his point as the others. But he spoke with passion and clarity. "Look at your own country. You started the war in Korea. Your soldiers are cruel and savage, no better than Hitler's troops or the Japanese who perpetrated one atrocity after another in China. Other imperialisms, Germany, England, France, have been so weakened by World War II that they are helpless. So the United States has taken over and is now determined to rule the world. The only thing that stops her are the great peace-loving nations of Russia, China, and the countries of eastern Europe. Your country, the United States of America, is creating war. Your leaders fear war, but they fear peace even more. You are controlled by a small group of selfish capitalists who have created a Fascist dictatorship. You have been helping that group. You are our enemy."

So the ranting at me and all I represented went on, day after day. Each day or so one of the G.G.'s would call me out to see if I was changing my mind. One day I was called for an official hearing. I sat on a low stool before a judge and his two secretaries from nine in the morning until five in the afternoon. We got nowhere. He asked me

221

what I had done over the years in China, and when I
stated that I had helped to send students to school, to keep
hospitals open, to preach the Gospel in city and country,
and to help in all types of social improvement, he blazed
away at me, declaring, "You are not sincere. You are not
telling the truth. Go back to your cell and keep studying,
for until you change your attitude and ideas, you cannot
see or speak the truth." He told me that they knew I was
an international spy of great importance, that a code message had been intercepted in the mails, and that until I
told the truth and repented of my anti-Communist attitude and actions, I could not be released. But first I must
see the light.

So I returned to my room and continued to study, to
listen to my "fellow students," and try to find some way
of presenting my case in language that the officials would
understand. The other prisoners warned me that I must
keep two facts at the forefront of my thinking. One was
that I must see my conduct, not from the Christian viewpoint, but from the Communist viewpoint. To talk religion meant nothing, for religion was an empty superstition.
What I had considered helpful to the Chinese people was,
from the Communist viewpoint, harmful. The second fact
was that it made no difference how serious my crimes had
been. The only thing that mattered was whether I repented and would stand with "the people" against the
reactionary forces of the world. Not what I had done, but

what I would do in the future—this was what counted. In other words, I must both repent and bring forth the fruits of repentance. Just as John the Baptist had preached, "Repent, for the kingdom of God is at hand," so the Communists preach, "Repent, for the kingdom of Communism is at hand." But the Communists, unlike John the Baptist, were not relying upon moral persuasion alone. They were using social pressure, applied patiently and continuously until they got results. If this did not work, they applied handcuffs and leg chains. It was a much more efficient, streamlined indoctrination than anything John the Baptist had thought of.

The learning came slowly and from many sources over the weeks. I read a dozen books, almost all of them in Chinese. I discussed problems with the group and learned the Communist phraseology. I listened to the G.G.'s as they criticized my attitudes and reactions. Gradually I acquired an elementary knowledge of Communism in the light of which I could present my problem and confess my crimes. Only then did I understand how they thought of me and the world in which we live.

The Communist doctrine is simple and convincing. All material things have within them a constant struggle that is resulting in constant change. This struggle and this change are for the better, a steady movement upward that finds its goal, historically, in the perfect society where scientific skills and socially motivated behavior will combine to create a heaven on earth, called "Communism." This constant change in material things, due to an inner struggle, is "dialectical materialism." It is materialistic because it assumes that change and progress are due to no outward spiritual forces, but are inherent in the character of matter itself.

Change and progress, due to inner struggle, are not only characteristic of matter; they are also basic in historical development. All history is a march upward, from a primitive communism up through the periods of slavery, of feudalism, of capitalism, and on to socialism where all of the tools and resources for production are socially owned. The three historical epochs of slavery, feudalism, and capitalism are characterized by the class struggle, the struggle between the few who possess power and oppress the people and the great body of laboring people who "have nothing to lose but their chains." The tools of production and the methods of production determine all social forms, religion, law, the state, education, and customs of every kind. Change those tools and those methods of production and you change the whole of society. Thus the central issue in every society is a matter of ownership and control of the tools of production and the natural resources—land, mines, forests, water power; these must be used, not for private profit but for public good.

In our own day, the struggle between the oppressors and the oppressed is sharpened because capitalism makes

224

possible an unprecedented concentration of power in the hands of a few. Capitalism inevitably creates imperialism, through which banking corporations, with the aid of political and military pressures, gain control over the colonial and semicolonial areas of the world. The struggles between capitalistic countries and between imperialistic powers and their colonies, plus the inevitable conflicts between capital and labor within the various countries, all combine to create that strife and uneasiness out of which wars grow. As long as we have imperialism, we shall have war.

But the Communist announces that the situation is not hopeless. On the one hand, the very stars in their courses fight on the side of change and progress. A new day is certain; it is written into the texture of the universe. But it is a day that awaits the united effort of man. Labor must awaken to the fact that the world can be changed. All society is the product of the labor of men, and there is no place for the parasitic capitalist that lives on the sweat of others. People must see clearly the class struggle and arise to defeat their oppressors. To recognize this onward march of history toward a socialized state, to believe that change is possible, to awaken to the sacredness of human labor, to join the proletariat in their struggle to overthrow the oppressive, ruling minority, and to dedicate all to the new day when all classes will be destroyed and men shall know equality, freedom, and plenty—this is to think in Communist terms. As we talked of the glorious new day of Communism that would soon be dawning in Russia, the faces of my fellow prisoners would light up with an enthusiasm not too different from that which illuminated my old grandfather's face when he talked of heaven. But he was basing his hopes on the infinite resources of an infinite God, while these prisoners were depending upon the very finite resources of blundering and sinning man. To me that makes a lot of difference.

But all of this Communist theory, this philosophy of "dialectical materialism," and its "historical materialism," was concentrated on the present world problems and was used to interpret the present international issues. To them today the United States has taken over the responsibilities of the old imperialisms of Europe, and is determined to bind all backward and colonial countries to the wheels of her chariot. The only thing that stands between America and her lust for power is Russia, a country which has found a new way of life that stands as a challenge and a threat to the capitalism of the West. So the United States, using the United Nations as her tool, is drawing a ring of steel around Russia and her friends, those who are doing their best to build a world of peace. The Korean war, launched by South Korea at the instigation of the United States, is just the first step in an attack upon China, and through China, upon Russia. The answer to such aggression must be a united Communist front in the Far East, plus the help of all of the "awakened people" in capitalist countries, all those who will oppose the fascistic and capitalistic groups that are making for war. For within Communism, all men who think alike are brothers.

Thus I learned what Communism is. I learned new words and new meanings for old words. I realized that until I could see my own conduct in the light of this new Communist teaching, there was no hope of clearing my case and being released from prison. For I had moved into a new land, and had to learn a new language. "Truth" was no longer a matter of scientific fact, but was only that which was in harmony with the needs and desires of "the awakened people." Anything that advances the revolution is "true"; all antirevolutionary thought is "false." True "democracy" is not that sham democracy of the West that is manipulated by the dictators of Wall Street and the Pentagon, but is the real control of society by the great mass of the farmers and industrial workers, operating through labor groups or soviets. Since the capitalistic minorities that have been defeated by the "people" may attempt a comeback, this democracy of the proletariat is a dictatorship of the proletariat in relation to their enemies. To be in prison was to feel the power of this dictatorship. The only way out of prison was to surrender, to bow to the will of "the people," and to give evidence that I would stand with the "enlightened people" in their struggle for a new world of Communism and peace. I need not sacrifice my Christian faith. But I must recognize the evils of imperialism and the wonder of the new way of life, and accept this as my way of life. To attempt to defend an alternative viewpoint or to take a middle-of-the-road position was impossible. For hatred and fear of America and all that I had represented was so deep that they had created a psychopathic condition in which all argument or free discussion was impossible.

So the training went on and so I moved over to the "people's platform." I admitted that my activities had been counterrevolutionary. I admitted that my speaking and writing had made the Chinese friendly to the United States and cool to revolutionary doctrine. I thought that that could be said of 95 per cent of the missionaries in China, and that if this was what they meant when they said I was a spy, then I would have to admit that I was a spy, a missionary spy. My fellow prisoners assured me that the more terrible my conduct and the greater my admission of guilt, the easier it would be for the government to believe that I had really reformed. So I dredged my experience to collect all the dirt I could to satisfy my judges. I told of pictures taken in city and country. I told of letters written to America, telling of conditions in China and supporting Chiang Kai-shek. I told of entertaining students and other friends in our home, and of lending them *Life* and other American magazines glorifying the capitalistic way of life. I admitted that I had distributed relief supplies. I con-

JOHN THE BAPTIST, STREAMLINED

fessed that I had hidden an American army rifle in an air-raid shelter behind my house, and told them where they might find it. This confession greatly strengthened their belief that I was telling the truth. I not only repented, but I brought forth the fruits of repentance.

But the most difficult problem was that "code message" which Pastor Judas had planted in some forged articles and mailed at the post office. I had to explain that. I had denied it for fourteen months, but I had no proof to support my denials. Therefore, I must be lying. So I admitted that I had sent that code, and explained all about it. That was a tough assignment, for it required a mystery story that would seem true to them. I created that kind of story, building it section by section, a mixture of truth and falsehood that had to be good enough to be convincing. I not only had to tell what was in the code, but build a story of spy organization and plots that sounded like a first-class thriller. I could not do it all at once, but moved slowly, making sure that I did not involve any Chinese friends and taking all blame upon my own shoulders or placing it upon organizations and individuals who were far away from Communist control. All situations or incidents which they could not check were given with great imaginative detail. All that they could check were reported as accurately but as vaguely as possible.

For many days the whole situation looked hopeless. I sat on the little stool before the judge hour after hour, listening to his long harangue and having nothing to give in return. I sat humbly in my corner night after night while the other prisoners told off my sins and the evils of American imperialism and the Chiang government, blaming me for everything they could think of. They blamed me for being so slow with my confessions. They did not know I was having to create my story as I went along. So

> Like little Jack Horner
> I sat in my corner
> Inventing many a lie;
> I altered all facts,
> All motives and acts,
> And confessed what a bad man am I.

At one point in this process, I got thoroughly sick of it all and revolted. I told two of the judges who had me out for questioning that I had been lying to them, and that my story was one long tale of fiction with little fact in it. They were horrified at my evident sincerity, and sent me back to my room to think about the matter again. An hour later one of them called me out again and said, "You cannot retract anything you have said. We will not let you. You have to go on from where you are." By that time I had recovered my nerve, given my conscience another dose of sleeping powder, and was ready to go ahead. Finally, the day came when the hearings were done, a summary of my evidence was drawn up, and after signing and finger-printing it, I was done.

I was done with the long hours of sitting before a judge. I was done with innumerable questions and listening to the endless harangue about my faults, my conservatism, my blindness to the "truth," and my stubborn refusal to reform. But I was not done with the problem of the rights and wrongs of my action. To this day I do not know whether what I did was "right" or "wrong."

At times I thought it would have been much easier to have dodged the whole issue. Several of my fellow prisoners had tried to do that. One had worked in the kitchen, and in an hour of emotional depression had tried to commit suicide. He had failed and was in our group, repenting of his mistake and getting re-educated. He slept next to me. Again and again I would note that he was sobbing in the night. Some other prisoner would note this, too, and then at the next mutual criticism meeting would try to compel him to tell his troubles. He refused to talk or tried to hide his true feelings. This only resulted in more criticism. I felt sorry for him, a lad from a farm, who had scraped through high school on a mere pittance and then had wasted several years vainly trying to get a job. He was homesick for father and mother and a little hillside farm. At one period I thought the lad was going insane. Another prisoner also had tried suicide. How many others had tried to escape in this way I did not know. But the officials were fully aware of this danger, and a strict rule forbade any prisoner to be left alone.

There must always be at least two prisoners together, each responsible for the other. I overheard one prisoner in an adjoining room cry out in agony, "But I want to die. I don't want to stay here." To which the official shouted in reply, "We will not permit you to die. You have got to reform. You'll reform or you will stay here until you rot." There was no way of escape.

Neither did Christian martyrdom seem feasible. If the issue had been clear cut, I could have faced martyrdom without flinching, not by my own strength but in God's power. I had had a vivid experience of that power in the third month of my solitary imprisonment. At that time the inquisitor had brought that code message to me for the first time, asserting that I had sent it, that it proved me a spy, and that the penalty for such an act was to face the firing squad. I replied, "I did not create that code, I never sent it, and I know nothing whatever about it." He thought I was lying, and warned me again that I was in grave danger. Looking him straight in the eye I said, "I know the penalty for being a spy in time of war. I never saw that code and know nothing about it. But if you don't believe me, I'm ready to march out to the execution ground right now." I said it quietly and with complete sincerity. As I said it I felt the sustaining power of God in a marvellous way. I could have walked out of there to death without turning a hair—not in my own strength but sustained by God.

Perhaps the issues that early Christians faced were clear cut, black or white. They had to renounce their Christian faith by worshiping at Caesar's shrine or lose their lives. It was Christ or Caesar. Before that kind of an issue the Christian can give only one reply. But I was confronting, not blacks and whites, but a muddy gray. The Communist prisoners and judges alike protested that the People's Government was not antireligious. My Christian faith was my private concern. I was in prison, not because I was a Christian, but because I had been the tool of Western imperialism. I was to learn later that Mr. Hung En-pu, principal of one of our high schools and an outstanding Christian, had been executed by the government. I later knew of other Christian friends who had committed suicide or had been shot. But in no case were they allowed to be martyrs to their Christian faith. In the eyes of the government and in all newspaper reports, all of them were criminals who had died because they were stubborn rebels against the people and dupes of China's enemies. I knew that soon after my arrest the papers had been full of the charges against me and that in the minds of all but a very small group of Chinese friends who had known me over the years, I was a foreign spy and an agent of American aggression in China. Anything that I said either to confirm or to deny these charges would have no effect upon the Chinese or the outside world. To have drawn a line, set my jaw in defiance, and in the spirit of Martin

Luther to have cried, "Here I stand—by God's help, I can do no other," would have been dramatic, but not good sense. Or so it seemed to me then.

Not only was the issue blurred, but the facts were equally mixed up. If I could have seen that the Communists were "all wrong" and our side, "all right," it would have been easier, easier for me then and easier now for all who think seriously upon the problems of our day. But the Chinese Communist line is not all false. When they talk of the evils of feudalism in China, the corruption of the Chiang government, the pressure of Western imperialisms upon China over the past hundred years or more, the race prejudice and economic injustice that blots the scutcheon of Christian America, the forces that are contributing to war, and the concrete accomplishments of the new People's Government in the fields of flood control, public health, mass education, and economic improvement, I could not help but agree. Probably the "facts" they cited to me were heavily loaded on the propaganda side. I knew that their picture of America, and even more their report of missionary work in China, was distorted and completely out of focus. But there was no value in arguing the matter. No facts that I could produce would be considered unless they confirmed the Communist view. They were completely right, and I was totally wrong. It was a one-package delivery. To refuse to accept their statement was not only to oppose the evil that I saw in their program, but it was also to deny the good they were doing. By stressing this good they contended that their program was in harmony with the social justice and concern for human betterment that is a part of my Christian faith. Thus to make an issue of the matter and to stand for my Christianity against their Communism was, in their eyes, to renounce the "social gospel" which, while far from being the whole of the Christian faith, is certainly a part of it.

To make the matter still more difficult, the judges were evidently sincerely desirous of helping me over the stile. They knew my difficulties. They knew that in terms of Christian idealism I was probably lying. But they were willy-nilly caught in the same system as I. I was in prison and could not leave my cell without the guard's consent. But they were under an equally stern, inflexible discipline. All the evidence they collected from me had to be processed through a committee. Unless my spoken and written statements satisfied this committee, they could do nothing. When I protested that I had not sent a letter or a telegram of which they accused me, they would reply, "Well, that may be so. But you admit that you sent others that were just as bad. It all amounts to the same thing. To admit this one is evidence you have really surrendered and are working with the people and not against them." To split hairs on such unimportant matters and to offend this affable Chinese official who was trying to help me out seemed unworthy of a Christian gentleman. I knew that what I said or signed would probably be used in propaganda, not against Christianity, but to support the war in Korea. But for that purpose the People's Government already had more than they could use.

Added to all of these factors was my deep conviction that God would lead me out of prison. Paul had had the same hope when in chains in Rome, and as far as we know, his hope was not fulfilled. He, as I, felt there was much to be done and that, if released, he could serve the Christian fellowship in a creative way. I, unlike Paul, had no chance to make a witness in prison nor to send out any letters from prison. What he or any other Christian disciple would have done if placed as I was, I do not know. I only know that it was a decision that had to be reached through a maze of truth and error, of gain and loss. I believe that through it all I held to my primary dedication to God's will for my life. I believe that out of it all will come a more valuable witness to His goodness and sustaining power than would have been possible if I had chosen some other course. But here, as in so many decisions in life, I am keenly sensitive to my own limitations of knowledge and insight, and can but pray that God will give me the faith to continue to walk ahead one step at a time and the humility to admit my own grievous blunders.

It is easy enough to say that I should have stuck to the

truth as I saw it. I had done that for fourteen months of solitary imprisonment and had convinced no one. All the language I used meant nothing. I remembered Jesus' words, "Do not give dogs what is sacred and do not throw pearls before swine." Evidently he had found, as I did, that there are those who have no appreciation of religious values and who cannot understand the truth when you speak it. To reiterate the truth before them is to waste your breath.

I thought of another statement of Jesus, found in Luke 12:11, 12, where Jesus says that when a disciple is dragged before the magistrate he is not to worry, "for the holy Spirit will teach you at that hour what you should say." I hesitate to affirm that this is true, for some of my literal-minded and argumentative friends will insist that the Spirit could not lead me to tell a lie. That is probably true. But it is also true that again and again when I had sat for hours on the little stool in front of the judge and could see no way out, a voice would say, "This is the key that unlocks the door. Say this and it will suffice." And it did. My prison mates complained that I was abnormal. As an international spy who might be taken out and shot the next day, I should have eaten little and slept less. But I ate like a pig and slept without waking. There was something the matter with me. I did not dare tell them that I left my troubles in God's hands, convinced that He would continue to "prepare a table before me in the presence of my enemies." One of the G.G.'s told me that I must not pray in prison. He might as well have ordered me to stop breathing.

After my case had been cleared, I had some six months or more of continued re-education or indoctrination, months of reading, discussion, and listening to the Chinese newspapers which were read daily. The final turn was to write out an accusation of America in which I denounced America for all of her sins. Much that I said was true, but it sounded like a drain inspector's report on American life. Economic injustice, race prejudice, war propaganda, corruption and waste—all of these exist in the United States, and in Communist eyes they are all that exist here. So I followed the Communist line and wrote of this side of American life, stating that there was also much that was good and that I would stand with "the great people" to build for peace, justice, and true democracy. They accepted this statement and at the end of nine and a half months permitted me to pack up my things.

What I had suffered over those months was no different from other prisoners. I was more fortunate than they in that I could create my mystery story with imaginary people and happenings in America, statements which the officials could not check, and involving people whom they could not interrogate. If a Chinese prisoner gave imaginary data, it would get him into serious difficulty, for his statements could all be verified. But the way in which our cases were handled was the same for all.

I knew little about my fellow prisoners, for the twenty commandments posted on the wall forbade our sharing the details of our problems or our backgrounds. But a certain amount of information leaked out. One prisoner sat next to me and whispered a good many secrets, facts about other prisoners and prison life in general. He had been in prison for more than a year. A graduate of Yenching University, interpreter for the Americans during the war against Japan, a correspondent, and after the Communists took Nanking and Shanghai, a student in the officers' training school at Nanking, he had seen a good deal. He had come out of a Christian home. With the outbreak of the war in Korea, the Communists had screened their seventy-five thousand students in the school at Nanking, taking about a thousand of them out because of their former association with the American military. He had been transferred to this prison for counterrevolutionaries at Chungking, had worn handcuffs and chains for forty days after his arrival, and now was serving out a sentence which he would only describe as "very long." He told me that all sentences ranged from three to twenty years, with a possibility of parole for those whose attitude and conduct were satisfactory.

The prisoners varied in their educational and social background. Several could neither read nor write. One boatman who had always lived a hard, vigorous life on the Yangtze River, sat in the corner crying like a baby. He said the officials were demanding information he did not have and that he had nothing more to confess. Denied all exercise outdoors, forced to listen hour after hour to discussions about Communist philosophy and economics which he could not understand, and even barred from joining in the games of Chinese chess which other prisoners played during the few hours of relaxation, his situation to him seemed hopeless. Another prisoner admitted that he had been a part of Chiang Kai-shek's spy organization, and that for nearly a year after arrest he had been stubborn in his refusal to talk. At the end of that time, he had seen the "truth" and had become convinced that the only road out of prison was by the way of complete confession. So he had told all he knew, implicating many others, and now hoped that he would be paroled within a year or so.

Sitting and sleeping next to me, and generously sharing some of his lice, was the former head of a normal college. He had had a checkered career. In the early twenties he had graduated at Shanghai and then returned to West China to lead in the Communist movement of those years. But with the ascendancy of Chiang Kai-shek, he had renounced his leftist friends and had become a member of the Nationalist party. His ability and loyalty were rewarded, and at the time of the Communist victory thirty years later, he had a place of considerable power and influence in the educational world. Now he was paying for his treachery to the Communist cause. At one time in his imprisonment he had been so hopeless that he tried to beat out his brains with a rock. He will wear the scars of this foolish attempt to his grave.

Most of the prisoners came from the middle class. There was one landlord, opium dealer, and lumber merchant by the name of Mr. Fang. He was an old man, over seventy. He had plenty of sins which he had confessed, and now was sitting out his imprisonment. He was a great asset to our discussion group. After each meal he would take out his dental plates, for which he boasted he had paid five millions of inflated Chinese currency, polish them off and wrap them up in a washcloth, and then be ready for action. The leader would call upon him for comment upon the subject at hand. With great impressiveness, he would repeat the most obvious facts in a dozen different ways, interspersing his remarks with plenty of "oh's" and "ah's," and move deliberately ahead to some clearly seen conclusion. Since the hours had to be filled with talk to convince the guards that we were working at our task of re-education, the long-winded members were highly prized. One prisoner stuttered, taking about twice as long to say anything as a normal person would. That helped out a lot. I was a disappointment, for my Chinese was not adequate to carry on long and colorful expositions. I would sum up my reactions on any subject in about three minutes, and then stop. Whereupon the leader in a discouraged tone would inquire, "Is that all?" My one value was that I could ask questions that others did not dare to ask, and then the day could be spent in setting me right. That was more fun for them than again digesting the predigested propaganda handed out in the newspapers.

Another prisoner had been an officer in the Nationalist regime, and his thumbnail sketch of his rise to power reflected the worst evils of the former government. His name was Hwang Tien-sui, or Mr. Yellow Heavenly-water. After finishing the sixth grade in West China, he had gone to Nanking for nine years in the officers' training school. Since graduation he had climbed to power by a wise choice of the right friends and by keeping out of all fighting at the front. He had ended his years of success by a period in Chungking, where as a major-general he had helped concoct false telegraphic reports to the Generalissimo about victories in Szechwan and had drawn the rice for sixty men to feed himself, his four wives, his twelve children, and his four bodyguards. Toward the end of the Japanese war, he had plotted with General Feng Yu-hsiang, the "Christian general," to take over power in the west when Chiang Kai-shek crashed. That plot had been liquidated when Chiang Kai-shek sent General Feng to the States on a long "vacation." The coming of the Communists had turned this major-general into a prisoner. Prisoner

Hwang was one of the few men I saw there who had had any relation to the Christian church. He said that he had first been a Protestant, then joined the Catholics, and now had turned to the "true faith" of Communism. The first two had not meant anything to him, by which he meant they had not increased his power and influence, and had not kept him out of jail.

I had a ringside seat at the "brain-washing" of one important prisoner. He was General Shang Chuang-i, former head of the Szechwan Provincial Assembly, trouble shooter for Chiang Kai-shek, owner of one thousand Chinese acres (about one hundred and sixty acres) of rich rice land, and husband of a brilliant wife who headed the Chengtu Electric Light Company and guided in a number of other commercial ventures. His oldest son, trained as a pilot in America, had lost his life in an air crash while flying for the Communists a few months after "liberation." So the "little general" was in prison, stripped of all wealth, power, and influence, and now facing the problem of admitting his crimes against "the enlightened people" and changing his thinking to fit in with the new regime. He was a tough nut, for he had a well-earned self-respect, the fruit of years of virtuous living. His Buddhist and Confucian faith was clear cut. He reflected the best of the old government, as Hwang had the worst.

But an impeccable character meant nothing to the Communists. In fact, the conscientious way in which he had served Chiang Kai-shek and the old order had made him an even more effective enemy of Communism. So he must change his mind and admit his crimes. His fellow prisoners worked on him day and night. Each member of the group would rant at him by the hour, pointing out his involvement in a decadent feudalism which had lived on the flesh and blood of a slave peasantry. Now the slaves were free and were in power. If the "little general" protested his innocence, the other prisoners shouted him down. All of the rottenness of the military and economic and political life of the old days was explained in lurid detail. Then he was told he was responsible for it, for he had upheld that rotten system. After some hours of such "education," he was ordered to confess what he was thinking. His confession contained a good deal of a self-exoneration, clear proof that he had not yet seen himself as a real criminal. So the group would start in again, lifting up some incident out of his personal history, interpreting it in the worst way, and laying all of the blame on him. There were long periods when he was compelled to stand up and listen to these tirades. There were three nights when the group split into two shifts and kept up a round-the-clock interrogation. Often the officials would come to the door and listen in, perhaps joining in the denunciation. Each day or so the leader would be called out to consult with one of the officials on the progress which we were making in changing the general's mind. Gradually he

244

changed. The facts had not changed any, and probably the government knew all there was to know before we ever saw him. But after some six weeks of this kind of pressure, General Shang could write pages and pages of detailed confessions of all that he had done over more than thirty years, not only giving the facts, but what was still more important, stating them so that all who read would know that he now saw he had been an enemy of the people. When I left the prison, he was still there. Probably he would be there for a long time.

How sincere my fellow prisoners were I do not know. I knew some of them were no more sincere in their confessions than I had been. They had to accept the new way of life, and were making their adjustment to it as best they could. Others were convinced that the Communist philosophy and the new People's Government would meet China's need and were in harmony with fundamental "truth." These had really had a conversion experience. But whether real or false, all prisoners were under constant surveillance both by their fellow prisoners and by the guards, and any rebellion would be noted and reported immediately.

The most interesting thing of those months of re-education was the daily reading of the Chinese newspapers. The paper we took was the official party paper, the *New China Daily News*. We read its four pages aloud from beginning to end, only skipping the few advertisements.

The news was meager, and the leading news item each day was accompanied by an official editorial, written at Peking, which gave the official interpretation of the news. All comment on the news followed the guidance of this editorial.

One thing I had to become accustomed to was the frequent "Selahs" that interrupted the even flow of all editorials and reports. In the King James Version of the Psalms, the word "Selah" appears every few verses. I long thought that this was the equivalent of "Amen." But scholars now say that this is a musical direction, and indicates at what points the horns and cymbals are to sound forth their glad acclaim. The equivalent in the Chinese papers is the unlimited praise of Mao Tze-tung, of the Communist party, and of Stalin. While I think that it is true that without the Communist party there could have been no new China, and that Mao Tze-tung will go down in history as one of the eight or ten most significant men of the twentieth century, this unadulterated praise is a bit annoying. We reserve such praise for God. But if you have no god, the only thing to do is to ascribe the attributes of deity to your earthly leader.

The newspapers are full of Communist teaching, of practical and helpful information and encouragement in the fields of public health, agricultural improvement, and industrial advance, and are designed to be used for serious study by discussion groups and individuals. The picture

of the outside world is warped. Eighteen millions unemployed in the States prove that a major economic debacle
is in the making and that the "enlightened people" will
soon rise to throw off their chains. When the election of
Eisenhower indicated this hope was hardly justified, they
just ignored the news. The Japanese elections were preceded by the same kind of optimistic prophecies, and then
no report was given of the results of the election. They
did not want to admit that twenty-two Communists had
been thrown out of the Japanese diet.

Hatred of America and reports of great victories in
Korea appear again and again. The United States soldier
is characterized by cowardice and cruelty. He even carries
a scalping knife with which he gleefully scalps his victims.
He is a poor fighter, and the Chinese volunteers are winning in every battle. The second year of the war resulted
in the killing of more than three hundred thousand U.N.
forces, of which one hundred and sixty thousand were
Americans. No report is made of the number of U.N. prisoners in North Korean hands and no one knows what
China is investing in the war, either in money or in men.
In the second year of the war some two hundred and
fifty millions was raised in voluntary subscriptions to support the war effort, an amount almost as large as the loan
secured from Russia. At the end of the second year, nearly
a thousand representatives, taking six thousand tons of
food and comfort supplies contributed from all over China,

247

went to Korea to encourage the volunteers at the front. As far as China knows, she is winning the war in Korea. No other report or interpretation is permitted in the press or over the radio.

On May 9, a G.G. came to the door of the room with a Chinese newspaper, one fourth of which was covered with photostatic copies of letters supposed to have been written by Kenneth L. Enoch and John Quinn, two American air officers shot down in Korea. In these letters they admitted that they had engaged in germ warfare. The G.G. asked me to read the letters, then translate them into Chinese for the group. When I read them, I turned to a prisoner next to me who could understand English and said, *sotto voce*, "Those boys are lying. They are members of my Ananias Club." But in Chinese I made no such statement, simply handing the stuff out to the group as it was written. The reason I knew those two airmen were lying was because they had followed the same technique that I had, giving plenty of details about meetings and individuals when such details had no real bearing on the matter of the germ bomb, and being very vague on any items that could be checked. Also, the idea that the United States military would spend millions of dollars on perfecting germ warfare, and then launch it at a time when, as the Chinese admit, the temperature stood at ten degrees below zero, is so patently absurd that no reasonable man could believe it. The Chinese knew this, and therefore

held up the news until May when people would have forgotten about the cold of the winter. In later statements
Enoch and Quinn gave details of the bombs they dropped,
Enoch even drawing a cross section of the bomb, a bomb
which he says he had never seen except in the dark as he
was getting into his plane. It is wonderful what the human
mind can do when Communist friends help you out. But
whether true or false, the germ propaganda was worth
all it cost the Chinese. For it increased anti-American hate
and at the same time made possible a very effective health
campaign of inoculation, vaccination, and cleanup that
stopped all plague and cholera in those areas which had
been devastated by the war.

Of the few Christian leaders whose names appeared in
the papers with any approval during the spring and summer of 1952, one was from England. He did not come to
China to preach the Gospel. If that had been his purpose
he would not have been admitted. He came to look at the
People's Government, with full assurance he would take
back an enthusiastic report of what he saw.

This visitor from England was Dean Hewlett Johnson,
and his wife. The "Red Dean" of Canterbury has been a
long-time friend of Russia and of the Communist group
in China. In his farewell speech at Peking, as in his report
upon his return to London, he told of the wonderful
progress that China is making in the fields of national
reconstruction. This report was largely true. He also said

that he had talked to scores of Christian leaders in China and had not found one who was not convinced the United States was engaging in germ warfare in Korea. That also was true, but it hardly proved that germ warfare was being used. It simply proved that the Chinese are living in a society where thought and speech are completely controlled by the government. China was at war. This war situation, plus the news controls that are tight in any dictatorship, Communist or otherwise, made it impossible for anyone to know or express any opinion at variance with the official propaganda line. Any pastor who was unwise enough to have openly doubted the statements of the papers would have been sent to prison for such reeducation as the government thought wise. Even in the United States during World War I, the atrocity stories that were manufactured by the war machine were accepted and repeated from many a pulpit. It is strange that Dr. Johnson did not realize that the same thing happens in China.

But, of course, Dr. Johnson could not read the Chinese papers. He could not read the long article that appeared condemning the Peking Union Medical College, in which doctors and nurses declared that this finest medical training center in China had killed thousands of patients by unjustified scientific experiments over the years. The medical staff had used peasants, rather than rats, for experimental purposes, because poor peasants were cheaper and more satisfactory material. He did not see the articles on Ling-nan University at Canton, where the foreign staff were all accused of acting as spies for the United States government and the one Catholic father on the staff was accused of spending his days in wine, women, and song. He did not read the confessions of great numbers of teachers in the universities who were marching forward with sickening uniformity to renounce all their connection with Western culture and to affirm that their years of service in the teaching profesion had been worse than wasted because they had not had the viewpoint of "the awakened people." If the good Dean had been able to read these papers and had seen how the Communists under the pressures of war and their own apologetic were blackening the name and besmirching the reputation of everyone who had had any contact with Western culture, he might have realized that the report on germ warfare was not as objective as he affirmed it was. These reports, like the germ warfare, all came out of the same propaganda spout.

Another propaganda weapon of first importance is the World Peace Congress, whose executive committee met in Berlin in the spring of 1952, and whose Far Eastern section held the Peace Conference for Asia and the Pacific Regions in Peking in early October. The Chinese government erected a seven-story building for a hostel for the several hundred guests who attended. It was a good show, and the guests who came were extended that warm hospitality for which China, whether capitalist or Communist, is justly famous. The tone of the Conference was set by Madame Soong Ching-ling, one of the vice-chairmen of China, and by Kuo Mo-jo, winner of the Stalin Peace Prize and one of the top officials in the Peking government. In summing up the results of the Conference, Kuo Mo-jo wrote that there had been perfect unanimity at the Conference. One delegate who had gone to sleep when a vote was taken was wakened up, briefed upon the matter at hand, and then the vote was taken again. It was a real peace conference, down to the last delegate, because everyone looked at all international problems through the same Communist lenses.

I read reams of speeches delivered at the Peace Conference in Europe and at the one for Asia and the Pacific regions. I could find no evidence in this Chinese material that any Communist country was in any way to blame for present world tensions. The representatives from Communist countries were often men in high positions in the Communist governments, and the whole statement of the problem of peace as reported in the Chinese press was nothing more than a reiteration of the Communist line. The expenditures in Communist countries for military matters, the number of troops under arms, the complete secrecy which surrounds all military affairs, and the complete abrogation of freedom of press and speech in these countries, all factors that contribute greatly to world tension, are wholly ignored. Capitalist countries are condemned for interfering in the internal affairs of other countries, but nothing is said about the "friendly help" Russia extended to those countries on her borders in Eastern Europe that they might establish their Communist governments. A loud cry is raised about the capitalist countries consulting together and planning mutual defense, but nothing about the visit of Chinese military representatives to Moscow. This is not to say that the Communist countries have no truth on their side. It is just to deny that all the truth is on their side. So the World Peace Congress meets year after year and erects its sounding board to proclaim many of the Communist doctrines on international affairs. These reports have a limited influence on the non-Communist world, but help to convince the Communist world, including China, that all the blame for world disorder is the fault of the other side. Which makes it a worth-while investment—for the Communists.

The long period of study, of indoctrination, of repeating the shibboleths of the Communist party came to an end. On the 8th of September I was given my final judgment. With kodaks clicking, this missionary spy stood before the judge while he read off my sentence—to be deported from China, to pay a fine of a couple of hundred dollars, and to write a summary of my confession. The departure was delayed by further charges that came in from a little town where we had a church, charges so absurd that the accusers could not make them stick. The fine was never collected. The confession consisted of a summary of the principal points in my case, written out by a Chinese official, and which I copied, closing with the sentence, "This is in my own handwriting; it is all my own." Finally, on November 8, just two months after the final judgment, I packed my suitcase, and under guard of two men, took boat to Hankow, train to Canton, and after a final day and night in the prison at Canton, was taken to the China border and released to go over into Hong Kong. I discovered that I was the last American Methodist missionary to leave China. Four Catholic fathers from Tibet traveled down under guard with me, but we were not allowed to speak to one another. I did not know until we crossed the border that one of them had sat in jail for more than three years. Comparing my experience with theirs and with others, I can only conclude that I had better treatment than was accorded to many.

In one of those closing days of imprisonment, a news item was read reporting that some criminal who had cut off his wife's head with the meat cleaver had been condemned to "an indeterminate prison sentence." I had never heard the Chinese term for that sentence before, *"wu ch'i t'u hsing,"* and, therefore, wanted to use it. So I remarked, "That's not very different from us. I, too, am serving 'an indeterminate prison sentence.'" The horrified protest of the group convinced me that I had certainly made a mistake that time. "It's a good thing that you are a foreigner and, therefore, to be excused for not knowing the language," declared one prisoner. "If we had said that, we would be put in chains. For we are not serving a prison sentence. We have had no final judgment. We are given a clean floor to sleep on, food as good as the average farmer has, a daily opportunity to learn the truth in study and discussion, a doctor when we are sick—and even free toilet paper if we cannot buy our own. To call this imprisonment is to doubt the good intentions of the government."

I admitted that I was wrong. It was only my Christian idealism that had noticed the bars at the windows, the armed guards at the door, the restrictions on movement and thought, and the weeks that kept accumulating until they added up to nearly two years, with no contact with the outside world. Now if I had been thoroughly reconstructed in thought-life and had been a true realist, I would never have noticed the prison bars nor the ranting of the judges and fellow prisoners. I would have realized that I was to be congratulated for living in the most wonderful country in the world, a country that had a glorious future second only to its great friend and leader, the U.S.S.R., a country where justice and freedom and new joy for all were blossoming forth under the beneficent sunshine of the great Mao Tze-tung, in a democratic society created by the marvellous work of the Communist party. Selah! It is strange how Christian idealism can lead one astray and trick one into subjective attitudes and judgments!

But that Christian idealism I cannot change now. My Christian faith goes too deep. After two years in Chinese Communist prisons, it is deeper than ever.

I flew from Hong Kong to Los Angeles to meet Esther on the 26th of November, exactly two years to the day since I had left her in 1950 to go off to jail in Chungking. And to be able to celebrate Christmas again in the States only served to deepen my idealistic prejudices. Yes, I continue to be an unregenerate and unrepentant idealist. Here is a Christmas meditation I wrote one July day in that hot Chungking cell:

> Ye magi who followed the distant gleam
> Of Bethlehem's guiding star,
> Did you ever have the faintest gleam
> It led to lands afar?
>
> Ye kings who prepared gifts to give
> To a Babe in manger stall
> Expressed the love whereby men live
> Who offer to Him their all.
>
> Ye seers who returned a secret way,
> Thus thwarting a despot's whim,
> Were but the first of many today
> Who risk their lives for Him.